Celebrating Soul

Marie-Louise von Franz, Honorary Patron

**Studies in Jungian Psychology
by Jungian Analysts**

Daryl Sharp, General Editor

Celebrating Soul
Preparing for the
New Religion

Lawrence W. Jaffe

To the memory of Edward F. Edinger, 1922-1998

Canadian Cataloguing in Publication Data

Jaffe, Lawrence W., 1931-
  Celebrating soul: preparing for the new religion

(Studies in Jungian psychology by Jungian analysts; 84)

Includes bibliographical references and index.

ISBN 978-0-919123-54-0

1. Jung, C.G. (Carl Gustav), 1875-1961.
2. Psychoanalysis and religion. 3. Spirituality.
I. Title. II. Series.

BF175.4.R44J325 1999   200'.1'9   C99-930319-8

INNER CITY BOOKS
Box 1271, Station Q, Toronto, ON M4T 2P4, Canada

Telephone (416) 927-0355 / FAX (416) 924-1814
Web site: www.inforamp.net/~icb / E-mail: icb@inforamp.net

Honorary Patron: Marie-Louise von Franz.
Publisher and General Editor: Daryl Sharp.
Senior Editor: V. Cowan.

INNER CITY BOOKS was founded in 1980 to promote the
understanding and practical application of the work of C.G. Jung.

Cover: "Miriam at the Well," monoprint by Vicki Cowan, © 1999.

Printed and bound in Canada by Thistle Printing Limited.

Contents

See final page for descriptions of other Inner City Books

Acknowledgments

Thanks to Dr. Harold Jaffe, Rev. Jeanne Sutter, Eleanor McKinney and to my editors Daryl Sharp and Victoria Cowan whose devoted and empathic work immeasurably improved the manuscript.

I am grateful for the support of the Ernst and Eleanor van Loben Sels Scholarship Fund and to the members of the Scholarship Committee of the C.G. Jung Institute of San Francisco, Millie Fortier, Kay Bradway and Brian Feldman.

Special thanks to my wife Susan C. Murphy for her editorial help, her understanding and her support.

Preface

We are living in an era of unparalleled impoverishment and depreciation of the human soul. The collapse of our religious forms has been followed by a general demoralization of the dominant (Western) culture. No myth remains to sustain us. The prevailing secular "religions" of humanism and rationalism prove inadequate because they fail to engage the transformative layer of our psyches.

The lack of a transpersonal belief system precludes the sense of community that many yearn for because ego-bound people have difficulty forming a vital, sustainable community. Community requires the sacrifice of selfish interests and this is only possible when such sacrifice is offered to something experienced as greater than the individual's ego. (It is then not even felt as a sacrifice.) This kind of belief is notably absent in our spiritually moribund society. Neither God nor country—no, and not "humanity" either—has the power to touch us to the core. All that remains is that most underrated entity of all, the individual soul.

People are beginning to bump up against the limits of materialism and rationalism, realizing that these fail to offer something essential, a purpose in life. (Man does not live by making a bundle alone.) Although a few turn back to institutional religion for orientation, many find that road barred to them by their reason and their skepticism. Whatever form the new religion takes it must leave a place, and a large one, for reason. The new religion will be the product of a marriage between reason and faith, science and religion. The closest approximation we have to this today is Jung's school of psychology, which affirms the redemptive power of consciousness.

We cannot do without meaning in our lives. Meaning cannot be established objectively; it arises only through a relationship with the inner, subjective world. But it is precisely that realm that has

7

been discredited in our day by the misapplication of the scientific spirit. In compensation I will describe and give examples of the inner life in order to help the reader sense *the reality of the soul.*

This book is an introduction to the spiritual as opposed to the clinical aspects of Jung's psychology. That C.G. Jung founded a school of psychoanalysis which bears his name is well known. Less well known is the fact that he created the framework for a new world view, which has been called the Jungian myth. My aim has been to put into personal and feeling terms the essence of this myth, namely its message of hope for a civilization which, as Jung said, has lost its sense of purpose and "forgotten why man's life should be sacrificial, that is, offered up to an idea greater than himself."[1]

Though divided into two parts, this book need not be read sequentially. It is meant to be entered at any point according to the impulse of the reader.

In Part One important theoretical terms are introduced and the plan of the book laid out. Part Two offers illustrations of how we can stay in touch with soul; each of these brief chapters is based on a "sacred" text, mostly from Jung or the Bible, translated into psychological terms.

---

[1] "Psychology and Religion," *Psychology and Religion,* CW 11, par. 133. (CW refers throughout to *The Collected Works of C.G. Jung)*

PART ONE
Theory

1
The New Religion

My name is Lawrence Jaffe. I am a Jungian analyst, which I define as a psychoanalyst with a spiritual bent.

To help us to recognize and reinforce the worth of the psyche (Latin for soul) is the primary aim of this book. In our materially oriented society it is easy to become hypnotized by the world of money and objects and to forget the riches of the inner world. We seem to need to be reminded each day of the value of our psyches. It is a function of prayer, and one of the goals of this book, to assist us in retaining our sense of connection with God. When I use the word "God" I mean it psychologically, as equivalent to the Jungian notion of the Self.[2] By "prayer" I mean any voluntary activity, including meditation, that reminds us of the reality of the psyche or evokes the ego-Self axis (below, page 27).

This book is actually three books in one:

1) Delineation of the new religion (Part One).

2) Devotions for the new religion (Part Two).

3) A possible central image or theme of the new religion, *the wounded inner child* (Parts One and Two).

Let us briefly look at these in turn.

Delineation of the New Religion

By "new religion" I do not mean Jungian psychology per se. I mean a new supreme value, an attitude of mind and heart bringing purpose and meaning to our spiritually bankrupt culture. The appearance of this new God or uniting principle coincides with the end of

---

[2] In Jung's model of the psyche, the Self is the archetype of wholeness and the regulating center, a transpersonal power that transcends the ego. Jung: "It might equally be called the 'God within us.' " *(Two Essays on Analytical Psychology,* CW 7, par. 399)

the New Testament era, approximately now, A.D. 2000. Discernible on the horizon are the first traces of light from a new sun, the new religion, whose central value is that of consciousness. Jungian psychology acknowledges and promotes this value in both the individual and the collective.

Although the first part of this book is specifically devoted to delineating aspects of the new religion, the reader may begin anywhere because capsule descriptions of it are scattered throughout.

Devotional Practices for the New Religion

This book had its inception in my own inability to stay in touch with the inner world despite my religious temperament and my vocation as a psychologist, both of which put me in daily contact with the eternal images. I realized how much more difficult it must be for those not so immersed in spirituality or psychology to retain connection to the reality of the psyche.

Over the centuries, traditional religions have developed forms to help us sustain our connection with soul, such as religious services, prayers and holy days, whereas those no longer contained in a living faith possess nothing comparable. I noticed that reading passages from Jung or the Bible frequently touched my heart, reminding me of the reality of the inner world. I decided to put together a compilation of such passages for my own use and that of others. Part two of this book is structured around these passages and appended commentaries, which I think of as "devotions" and which are meant to recall us to the inner world, the dwelling place of soul.

Rather than a linear arrangement, the form of this book is spiral or circular and includes the repetition of key concepts. This structure permits access at the pleasure of the reader.

**The Wounded Inner Child: A Possible Central Image
of the New Religion**

The image of the child is a very common symbol for an emerging highest value or organizing principle in the psyche. Examples from the Judeo-Christian myth include the Christ child and Moses in the bulrushes. Hence we should not be surprised at the appearance of the child motif at the start of a new era such as the one we are now approaching.

The image of the child and especially the wounded child seems to grant direct access to our soul. As Wordsworth noted, "clouds of glory" trail behind a new baby or young child.[3] We readily sense the presence of a god.

Subjectively, we have readier access to the inner child than to other inner personalities (such as the mother within or the criminal within) perhaps because we remember ourselves as children; perhaps, too, because children usually arouse positive feelings and are identified with hope and the future.

The inner child grants us an experience of the hidden value of the inner world, and it is crucial that the inner world become real to us—that is what is meant by *the reality of the psyche*. References to the wounded inner child are scattered throughout the book. It is my hope that some of the commentaries will put us in touch with our wounded souls and provide meaning for our suffering.

*

Because of an unempathic early environment I was driven as a child to try to understand myself—nobody else seemed to. Because the outer world (represented by my family), misunderstood me I sought solace in its compensation, the inner world. In former times I might have become a rabbi but because neither temple nor church services moved me, I turned to psychology in an effort to understand myself, realizing only much later that the impulse to understand myself was a religious one.

As a Jungian analyst I have worked daily with people who, like myself, had been traumatized in childhood and had unconsciously striven to compensate for that wounding in a variety of ways: neu-

---

[3] "Ode: Intimations of Immortality from Recollections of Early Childhood," in *Poetical Works,* p. 460.

rosis, religion, sexual acting out, substance abuse, overeating, overwork, devotion to "isms," criminality, rationality and, most common of all, a search for a feeling of worth through love.

I discovered, along with my patients, the painful fact that an intimate adult relationship failed to repair the childhood deprivation of love and empathy. Surprisingly, neither did money or fame. The deprivation could be healed only through a change in a person's relationship to his or her own wounded inner child, and I came to believe that this process is a major task of therapy.

Nearly everyone is subject to childhood emotional trauma which, if not confronted by consciousness, determines one's fate. The Jungian myth represents a compensation for that universal wounding. Raising those wounds to consciousness (by reexperiencing them emotionally) liberates us from the compulsive influence of the complex. In other words, awareness of the wounded inner child has a healing effect.

The tools for this life-saving work of bringing consciousness to bear on unconscious childhood patterns (that is, complexes) have been developed by such theoreticians as Freud, Heinz Kohut and D.W. Winnicott. What, then, is Jung's contribution?

For some patients, myself included, Jung puts in perspective the whole experience of wounding in childhood and partial healing in adulthood. Since the experience of wounding is nearly universal it must convey universal significance. Without intending it, parents deal deadly wounds to the children they love. The children later repeat the pattern with their own children. Consciousness alone has the power to break that tragic cycle. Jung wrote that "the enlightened human consciousness breaks the chain of suffering and thereby acquires a metaphysical and cosmic significance."[4]

Consciousness is discussed at length in the next section. The expression "chain of suffering" refers to the fact that we do unto others what was done unto us. This usually occurs so naturally, spon-

---

[4] *Letters*, vol. 2, p. 311 (modified).

taneously and unconsciously that our children are grown before we realize the damage we have inflicted. It is written that the sins of the fathers are visited upon the sons "unto the third and fourth generation."[5] But if we raise our woundings to consciousness we spare our children, lovers and friends, at least in some measure, from the poisonous sting of the viper that wounded us.

Although techniques exist for raising childhood traumas to consciousness without recourse to Jungian ideas, some people require a broader context in which to place this whole tragic cycle of being hurt and hurting others. In other words, a knowledge of the meaning of our sufferings may give us the courage to bear them. This is the point where an acquaintance with Jung becomes helpful.

Meaning has always been the domain of religion, but for many today the traditional religions no longer offer orientation and guidance. We who have lost our religious moorings lack the tools to compensate for the overwhelming power of society and the material universe. Defeats in the outer world may assume exaggerated importance because the outer world measures success chiefly in terms of accumulating money and pleasure. As Fagin sings in the musical version of *Oliver Twist*, "In this world, one thing counts / In the bank, large amounts." And the modern rapper concurs: "It's all about money / Ain't a damn thing funny."[6]

If we are injured in our bank account or our self-esteem, or suffer disappointment in love, we may find little inner consolation. This is especially likely if we have been traumatized as children. Along with our religion we have lost the certainty of our place at the center of the universe. We are no longer confident that the hairs of our head are all numbered or that no sparrow will fall to earth

---

[5] Exod. 20:5. (Biblical quotations throughout are from the Authorized King James Version, unless otherwise noted.) Interpreted psychologically this passage suggests that as far back as we can reckon (generally no more than three or four generations, but, symbolically, *indefinitely*) parents have unwittingly infected their children with the family myths and complexes.

[6] Grandmaster Flash and the Furious 5, "The Message," © Priority Records, 1989.

without our Father's will.[7]

Let us pursue for a moment the example of money. People nowadays become alarmed if the latest statistics show a slight increase in the proportion of the population below the poverty line. For our forebears for whom the Judeo-Christian myth was still vital and sustaining, the knowledge that they were children of God compensated for their poverty. Poverty implied no personal shortcoming, merely one's lot in life, mostly inherited—like gender, say, or eye color. In this era of the death of God one can no longer be poor with dignity.[8] Money is the measure of our worth. In the absence of a living religion nothing but prosperity can compensate for poverty.

A new myth is required and this has been provided by Jung, who reinterpreted traditional religious images psychologically and experientially. This yields a double boon. It revivifies the religious imagery by understanding it in the light of reason, and it adds feeling to our scientific view of the world. In other words Jung has helped forge a bridge between science and religion, logos and eros, head and heart; that bridge is depth psychology.

We are in the first stages of a collective movement of the spirit, similar to the first four hundred years A.D. when Christianity displaced paganism in Europe. The current change in consciousness we call the Psychological Dispensation.[9]

According to Joachim of Flora, there have been three periods of world history: the Age of the Law, or of the Father; the Age of the

---

[7] Matt. 10:29; Luke 12:6.

[8] By "death of God" I mean His absence as a living presence in the lives of most modern people. The subjective fact of the "death of God" does not necessarily contradict theological constructs of an immortal, transcendental God. Nor is this "death" necessarily relevant to the East, which is living under the sway of a different myth than the Judeo-Christian/Greek myth of the West.

[9] By "dispensation" I mean the form in which a thing is dispensed or distributed. Just as water, for instance, can be dispensed via tap, ladle or cupped hands, the spirit can be dispensed in various ways. According to Joachim of Flora's idea (elaborated upon by Jung and Edward F. Edinger), the spirit, too, can be dispensed in various guises or "dispensations."

Gospel, or of the Son; and the age we are now entering, the Age of Contemplation or of the Holy Spirit.

In the first age, the Hebrew Dispensation, God chose a group of people, the Israelites. In the second age, the Christian Dispensation, God chose a single individual, his firstborn, Jesus Christ. In the age we are now entering, the Psychological Dispensation, God is incarnating in each of us individually. We are each called upon to bear the burden of being special to God. Depth psychology names this process *individuation*.

Hearing the call of God is not an unalloyed blessing. If you get nothing more out of this book than a glimpse of the paradoxical nature of the God-image as experienced psychologically your effort will have been rewarded. Every content of the unconscious as it emerges into consciousness is seen to have a double aspect, i.e., a good and a bad side—a sea of grace meets a seething river of fire. Individuation, then, is not necessarily an attractive fate though, on the other hand, it may offer a sense of fulfillment as reflected in Jesus' words, "I . . . finished the work that you gave me to do."[10]

Despite its potential rewards, few of us embark upon the path of individuation willingly. The last thing the Western mind wishes is to look at itself. We only do so when we have no alternative. A glance at the history of the Jews or the life of Christ reveals what is in store for the individuating person: on the one hand, chosenness—a sense of being special to God and fulfilling God's purposes; but, on the other hand, misunderstanding and persecution. Chosenness and persecution are part of the same archetype—you can't have one without the other.

Individuation is a calling imposed upon us as surely as it was imposed upon the Jews and upon Christ. It is valuable to God but neither restful nor comfortable. To live well and naturally, our lives, paradoxically, must be sacrificial, that is, devoted to something greater than our own ego.

---

[10] John 17:4, Jerusalem Bible.

*

I dreamed many years ago that I had inhaled poison gas and would soon die. My wish was to spend my last days in Jung's service. In the dream his wife advised me that my task would be to carry his baggage.

In the ensuing years I have come to understand this dream as assigning me the task of helping carry forward Jung's message, which, largely unheeded during his lifetime, became such a burden to him. His despair is reflected in the following passage, recorded six months before his death.

> I had to understand that I was unable to make the people see what I am after. I am practically alone. There are a few who understand this and that but almost nobody sees the whole. . . . I have failed in my foremost task: to open people's eyes to the fact that man has a soul and there is a treasure buried in the field and that our religion and philosophy are in a lamentable state.[11]

Jung failed in his self-appointed task because of the difficulty, in this extraverted society, of retaining in consciousness the reality of the psyche. Collective forms like churches, rituals, holy days, liturgies, canonical laws, prayers, sabbaths, jubilees, church calendars, books of hours, devotional works of art, literature and music—most of these no longer help us to keep in mind the reality of the soul. Perhaps some of those relics of the Hebrew and Christian Dispensations can be modified to work in the age of the new religion that we are now entering, namely the Psychological Dispensation.

I realize that the word "dispensation" has dogmatic overtones. It refers to the specific arrangement or system by which our perception of the world is ordered. This evolves over time, hence the sequence Hebrew Dispensation, Christian Dispensation, Psychological Dispensation.[12]

---

[11] Quoted by Gerhard Adler, "Aspects of Jung's Personality and Work," in *Psychological Perspectives,* vol. 6, no. 1 (Spring 1975), p.14.

[12] It is important to note that previous dispensations are not extinguished; rather

Because no collective forms yet exist to help us remain conscious of the reality of the inner world (the soul), each of us must provide our own tabernacle (structure) in anticipation of the day when enlightened communities will arise to assume that function. In fact, such an institution has already arisen, depth psychotherapy, which prepares us to understand Jung's insights. In other words, the experience of depth psychotherapy, because it represents an encounter with the inner world, prepares us to understand the language of the soul (unconscious). Another modern structure which apparently aids many in the process of individuation is the Twelve Step Program, practiced for example in Alcoholics Anonymous, which (though this is not widely known) Jung was instrumental in helping to found.[13]

Before the birth of depth psychology it was religion alone which occupied itself with a proper relationship to the unconscious, which for the religious meant God. Religion devoted itself to the question of how human beings are to come to terms with the principalities and powers of the unconscious. With the discovery of the unconscious as a scientific datum in the late nineteenth century by Freud, Jung and others, a new era was inaugurated where the unconscious (the image of God) became a subject of scientific inquiry.

The way we see the world is governed by the unconscious, not the ego. Jung's view differs, in this respect, from the popular notion, implicit in most New Age thinking, that we are free to choose who we are. The Jungian idea is that the sovereignty of the ego is limited but that it may enter into dialogue with the unconscious and even influence it through the development of consciousness. In

---

each successive revelation or mutation builds upon its predecessors in an evolutionary spiral.

[13] In a letter to Bill W. (a co-founder of A.A.) Jung wrote of his patient, a friend of Bill W.'s, "His craving for alcohol was the equivalent, on a low level, of the spiritual thirst of our being for wholeness; expressed in medieval language: the union with God." The exchange of letters between Jung and Bill W. is reprinted in Jan Bauer, *Alcoholism and Women: The Background and the Psychology*, pp. 123ff.

Western culture, one of the main tools we have for this process today is depth psychotherapy.

The first phase of psychic transformation involves insight. The second phase involves changing habits which, because they function autonomously, are resistant to modification through the intervention of the conscious mind. Although new patterns of behavior sometimes supplant the old patterns without conscious effort, often they require an assist from the ego. The regular practice of prayer can help in the process of psychic transformation both by bringing forth and by establishing new attitudes and behaviors.

Prayer may resemble what Jungians call active imagination, which may involve writing, painting, drawing or sculpting. The subject of a painting, for instance, could be an image from a dream or even a mood or feeling. Alternatively, one could paint or sculpt or write with no conscious purpose except to allow the unconscious to speak. Active imagination could also include guided meditation, movement, dancing, singing or playing an instrument. Through attending to images in the psyche and expressing them in a definite form, active imagination facilitates the dialogue between ego and unconscious and thereby the process of individuation.[14]

The prayer or active imagination I will be talking about in this book, however, is limited to contemplation of the written word. In the Western tradition this is the most common type of prayer, often being recited aloud in houses of worship. Because for many of us the life has gone out of these traditional religious services, a new form of prayer must be developed. I hope this volume will be a contribution to that process.

This book, then, is meant to supplement the process of depth psychotherapy by highlighting some texts, mostly from Jung and the Bible, which may help us to keep in mind the reality of the inner world. The selections are highly personal. They are words that have lighted *my* darkness, soothed and spoken to *me*. The reader

---

[14] Robert Johnson has written an important book on this subject called *Inner Work.*

must discover the words that touch him or her. This book is intended as testimony, example and a beginning for *you*.

Newspapers, magazines and books are filled with advice on how to make our lives more efficient. The trouble is that modern life has become a business that can easily eat up all of our time. This book reminds us of the other, almost forgotten world we also inhabit, which has many names: eternal world, psyche, inner world, soul.

2
The Jungian Myth

If you understand the supreme value of awareness, you understand the Jungian myth. Note that "myth" is understood here psychologically, as a "living structure or container that conveys a sense of a connection to a transpersonal level of existence."[15]

One way to catch a glimpse of the Jungian myth is to consider that *witnessing* has the power to transform what is witnessed. For example, patients often speak of their childhood woundings. If witnessed compassionately by the therapist, patients can, in time, release their burdens of hurt, anger and hatred. This is an example of the world-redeeming power of consciousness.

In order to communicate Jung's myth for modern individuals, I am going to say much the same thing in different ways in the hope that a particular formulation will click.

The Jungian myth affirms the centrality of the process of individuation. Here are three definitions of individuation, each accompanied by a short explanation. Perhaps one or more will communicate something to individual readers.

1) *Individuation is the life-long process of becoming a conscious individual.*

This is individuation defined in its simplest terms. The purpose of human life, according to Jung, is to serve God by generating consciousness.

2) *Each one of us must discover the place in this world which, for good or ill, we are intended to fill according to our own nature.*

This definition emphasizes the unique fate that the individuation process holds in store for us. Knowledge of that unique fate is

---

[15] Edward F. Edinger, *An American Jungian: Edward F. Edinger in Conversation with Lawrence Jaffe,* tape 3.

rarely granted us as a gift; it must be discovered, and that usually happens only through painful trial and error.

3) *Individuation is the continuing incarnation of God for the purpose of divine transformation.*[16]

This is the most pregnant of the definitions because it emphasizes the role of the Self (God) in the process of individuation. Like the first definition, it suggests that consciousness contributes to the evolution and differentiation of the God-image.

*

The central idea of the Jungian myth is the redemptive power of consciousness. This idea can be summarized with two quotations 2,000 years apart:

When a man knows himself he knows God.[17]

Whoever knows God has an effect on him.[18]

Combining these we have:

If we know ourselves we have an effect on God.

The relationship between the Jungian myth and depth psychotherapy now becomes clear, because depth psychotherapy promotes knowledge of ourselves more effectively than any other modern institution. Psychotherapy is an invention of the twentieth century; religions were the earliest psychotherapeutic systems.

The Nature of Consciousness

The expression "new religion" refers to a new highest value, consciousness, which will come to prominence in the age we are now entering. A major tenet of the new religion is that our human attempt to be as aware as possible contributes to the evolution and differentiation of the God-image.

---

[16] Edward F. Edinger, personal communication.

[17] Clement of Alexandria, *Paedagogus*, III, 1, quoted by Jung in *Aion*, CW 9ii, par. 347.

[18] "Answer to Job," *Psychology and Religion*, CW 11, par. 617.

Psychologically, God-image and God cannot be distinguished because scientific statements can be made only about things we have experienced in some fashion. Statements about the transcendent God in his ultimate reality are outside the realm of the science of psychology. As a psychologist I attempt, from an empirical frame of reference, to reconcile science with religion and thereby carry forward the work of C.G. Jung.

The new religion is more individual than traditional religions and less dependent upon faith, ritual and dogma. It places its emphasis upon the careful consideration of personal subjective experience, that is, consciousness. As Socrates observed, "The unexamined life is not worth living."[19]

So far, the Psychological Dispensation, the new religion of consciousness, has one major ritual—depth psychotherapy. Psychotherapy can in fact be understood as the successor to religion in the high value it places on subjective experience, especially feeling. One etymological root of the word "religion" is Latin *religio*, meaning "careful consideration," which is appropriate because religion, like depth psychotherapy, assigns value to subjective states and expects a boon from attention to such phenomena as memories, dreams, fantasies, moods and feelings. One hoped-for result of both psychotherapy and religion is that the patient/devotee will forge a connection to a power greater than the ego. Jung's term for this power is the Self. The religious term is God. A relation to the Self grants us an indestructible inner authority.

*

The Jungian myth posits that the consciousness we achieve in our lives is redemptive. Consciousness or awareness affects not only those close to us but, mysteriously, the whole world: past, present and future. We share the same nature as the cosmos and exert an ongoing and reciprocal influence upon it. Hence our conscious-

---

[19] Plato, *Apology,* in *The Works of Plato,* p. 129.

ness has an effect on the unknown background of the cosmos (God, or in psychological terms, the unconscious). Just as God affects us, we affect God.

This process is called *transformation of the God-image,* of which the essential ingredient is consciousness. Human consciousness appears to have a specific stimulating and invigorating effect upon the unconscious. The idea that God takes a personal interest in human beings with whom He maintains an ongoing dialogue is the essential contribution of the Jews to human history. This idea was taken up by Christianity and is coming to fruition now in the Psychological Dispensation, where the idea that something can change in the unconscious (God) as a result of attention being directed to it is the basis of depth psychotherapy.

*

Consciousness should not be misunderstood as something purely intellectual. Like "conscience" it derives from the Latin roots *con,* meaning "with," and *scire,* meaning "to know." Therefore consciousness signifies "knowing with" an "other." The other may be God or another person or another part of ourselves like the wounded child. Consciousness combines head (logos) and heart (eros). This contrasts with "science" which is derived from *scire* alone and therefore denotes pure knowledge detached from feeling or "withness." Jung writes, "He who loves God will know God."[20] This is the sort of knowledge, driven by the heart, which is the bedrock of consciousness.

Edward F. Edinger writes,

On the collective level, consciousness is the name for a new supreme value coming to birth in modern man. The pursuit of consciousness, "con-science," unites the goals of the two previous stages of Western history, namely religion and science. Religion (meaning "linking back") has as its essential purpose the maintaining of man's connectedness with God. This corresponds to Eros, the

---

[20] "Answer to Job," *Psychology and Religion,* CW 11, par. 732.

connecting principle, and the "withness" factor of consciousness as "knowing with." Science, on the other hand, boldly gave up the connection with the other and opted instead to pursue an increase in human knowledge. If religion is Self-oriented, science is ego-oriented. Religion is based on Eros, science on Logos. The age now dawning will provide a synthesis for this thesis and antithesis. Religion sought linkage, science sought knowledge. The new worldview will seek *linked knowledge.*[21]

*

The expression "Jungian myth" refers to the idea that the transformation of the God-image depends on human consciousness. In its simplest form it can be represented by the following diagram, which shows the relationship between the ego, the center of the conscious personality, and the Self, which includes both the unconscious and the conscious personality.[22] Remember, the relationship between ego and Self corresponds to the relationship between man and God.

Stages of Ego Development

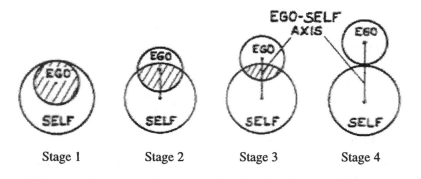

| Stage 1 | Stage 2 | Stage 3 | Stage 4 |

Stage 1: This is the state of the ego prior to the expulsion from paradise. In the garden of Eden ego and Self are one—which means

---

[21] *The Creation of Consciousness: Jung's Myth for Modern Man,* pp. 57f.
[22] Reproduced from Edinger, *Ego and Archetype: Individuation and the Religious Function of the Psyche,* p. 5.

there is no ego. When there is no separation between ego and Self there is no dialogue; neither can there be relationship. To merge means to lose consciousness.

Stage 2: This is the state of Adam's consciousness after the expulsion from Paradise. It depicts, as well, the general level of consciousness up to modern times. The ego is emerging from containment in the Self but has its center and greater area in the Self.

Stage 3: This is the state of consciousness in the coming age. The ego-Self axis has now become partly conscious. It is in this stage that God is born in human consciousness.

> God is a consequence of consciousness. He is born in the human soul and he doesn't exist until he's born—as in the Nativity of Christ.[23]

Stage 4: This is an ideal state of consciousness—a total separation of ego and Self and a complete consciousness of the ego-Self axis. It may not exist in reality, but it is included here for the sake of theoretical completeness.[24]

Transformation of the God-image

To help us to understand what is meant by the transformation of God (the evolution and differentiation of the God-image) Edinger offers a simile: The God-image is like the atmosphere, the pervasive medium in which we exist but of which we are unaware. We participate in it. It is inside and outside of us. It expresses itself through us. Because we are of the same substance as it, it changes as we change.

The God-image is the main content of the objective psyche—the pervasive medium within which we live out our whole lives. It is like water is for fish. Edinger likes to pose this riddle: "Who dis-

---

[23] Edward F. Edinger, *Lectures on Jung's* Aion, tape 10. See also Edinger, *The Aion Lectures: Exploring the Self in C.G. Jung's* Aion, p. 147.

[24] For further commentary on these stages of ego development, see Edinger, *Ego and Archetype,* pp. 5ff.

covered water?" Answer: "I don't know, but it wasn't the fish."[25] What we swim around in and what contains us and sustains us is invisible to us.

Jung was arguably the first to crawl out of the deep and glimpse, as he struggled to draw breath, what had contained him, the objective psyche. According to Edinger, Jung is an "epochal man," that is, "a man whose life inaugurates a new age in cultural history," or alternatively, "the first to experience and to articulate fully a new mode of existence."[26]

Just as Christ was the first Piscean man, so Jung was the first Aquarian man. In the Piscean age we swam in the waters of the unconscious which sustained us. (The unconscious is often symbolized in dreams by the ocean.) In the Aquarian age our relationship to the waters is becoming more conscious. As the image of Aquarius tells us, we are fated to assume the burden of the unconscious upon our shoulders.[27]

The way in which God needs to be seen and acknowledged or worshipped resembles an infant's need to be seen by its mother, or our own need to be seen or mirrored by our lover. We embody consciousness and every being in the world cries out for human consciousness because only in the light of consciousness (which, remember, combines knowing and relatedness) can any of God's creatures bloom and attain the beauty that is their birthright. This is

---

[25] *Lectures on Jung's* Aion, audiotape.

[26] *Creation of Consciousness*, p. 12.

[27] At the beginning of the Christian era, about 2,000 years ago, the vernal equinox entered the zodiacal house of Pisces (fish) and is now on the point of entering Aquarius (water bearer). This apparent movement of the sun is known to astronomy as the precession of the equinoxes: a slow westward shift of the equinoxes along the plane of the ecliptic resulting from the conical motion of the earth's axis of rotation. A complete cycle requires about 26,000 years, roughly 2,000 years for each of the twelve Zodiac signs. Qualities of our unconscious are projected upon the heavens, thus the Zodiac becomes the basis for astrology. Jung writes that time "proves to be a stream of energy filled with qualities and not, as our philosophy would have it, an abstract concept." (*Letters*, vol. 1, p. 139)

readily seen in the young child who visibly thrives and glows in the presence of admiring attention.

The Old Testament not only documents our dependence on God but also chronicles God's need for us to acknowledge, respect and validate Him, and His rage when He feels He is not getting the recognition which is due Him. Then He may destroy the world—just as some of us feel we could annihilate the one who has invalidated or humiliated us or treated us unjustly.

We sometimes call this "narcissistic rage," and I do think some of us who have had our feeling of worth undermined in childhood are more sensitive to feelings of being robbed of our dignity in adulthood. Nor do I think these feelings are confined to those we label as narcissistic. I would like to substitute for narcissistic the expression "wounded in the self" (the ego-self). The weakened sense of self that some people suffer from as a result of their childhood injuries and the rage they may feel when their sense of self is threatened with fragmentation corresponds to the rage of the Old Testament God, Yahweh.

Just as God cannot be unless man gains enough consciousness to perceive Him, the ego cannot be unless someone perceives it. No person can be unless someone else has gained enough consciousness to recognize an aspect of that person's essential nature. If you understand someone, even if you never speak a word, you have an effect on that person's unconscious—that is an essential mechanism of psychotherapy.

An alternative way of comprehending this very difficult idea of the transformation of the God-image is to consider the biologist Rupert Sheldrake's hypothesis of "morphic resonance." According to this idea the form and behavior of plants and animals can be modified "by the form and behavior of *past* organisms of the same species through direct connections across both *space* and time."[28]

An example of morphic resonance is the observation that if rats

---

[28] *A New Science of Life: The Hypothesis of Formative Causation,* back cover.

in Kansas, say, are trained to negotiate a new and difficult maze, rats in London, England, will require fewer trials to master it. It is not that the British rats have more native intelligence, but presumably the learning breakthrough achieved by the Kansas rats is somehow communicated to their cousins abroad. There is considerable evidence both anecdotal and experimental to support Sheldrake's theory, which is elaborated and refined far more than I have space to convey here.

Another example, from the inanimate world, is the greater difficulty in crystallizing a chemical for the first time than on subsequent occasions. Once a chemical is crystallized in Australia, say, it is far easier to crystallize it in Milan even in the absence of communication between the two laboratories.

Sheldrake's hypothesis implies that whereas it is with difficulty that a form or event appears for the first time in history, the likelihood that it will recur improves enormously after the first instance. This idea is relevant because it suggests that changes in the collective psyche can be brought about by changes in the consciousness of individuals.

My own experience is that in a successful psychoanalysis not just the ego changes; the unconscious changes too, in response. This change in the psychic background is what is meant by the transformation of God or the God-image.

3
Jungian Spirituality

Only the living presence of the eternal images can lend the human psyche a dignity which makes it morally possible for a man to stand by his own soul, and be convinced that it is worth his while to persevere with it. Only then will he realize that the conflict is *in him,* that the discord and tribulation are his riches, which should not be squandered by attacking others; and that, if fate should exact a debt from him in the form of guilt, it is a debt to himself. Then he will recognize the worth of his psyche, for nobody can owe a debt to a mere nothing.

. . . . If the projected conflict is to be healed, it must return into the psyche of the individual, where it had its unconscious beginnings. He must celebrate a Last Supper with himself, and eat his own flesh and drink his own blood; which means that he must recognize and accept the other in himself. . . . Is this perhaps the meaning of Christ's teaching, that each must bear his own cross? For if you have to endure yourself, how will you be able to rend others also?[29]

I will consider the above passage bit by bit, in order to illustrate the substance of Jungian spirituality. First:

Only the living presence of the eternal images can lend the human psyche a dignity which makes it morally possible for a man to stand by his own soul, and be convinced that it is worth his while to persevere with it.

The eternal images correspond to what humanity has always called God. Because the image of God is produced in all times and places by the psyche it represents a scientific or phenomenological datum. The nature of God in his external reality is a subject for theology, not for science. I use the terms God and God-image inter-

---

[29] *Mysterium Coniunctionis,* CW 14, pars. 511f.

changeably because, scientifically speaking, all we can know of God is His image in the psyche.

For the benefit of many modern people who have no strong sense of what is meant by God, I will explore the idea in the following paragraphs.

God is unknown by definition because God is just that which falls *outside* the bounds of the ego (the conscious mind). We cannot comprehend God; God comprehends us. Notwithstanding, if the reader can recall encounters with a power greater than his or her ego in the form of accidents (fortunate or otherwise), symptoms, closeness to death, love or hate, dreams, visions, or experiences of nature—then he or she may have had an experience of what Jungians call the Self, the God-image in the psyche.

When Jung was asked if he believed in God he paused and then replied, "I *know*. I don't need to believe. I know."[30] What he meant was, "I know, through my own experience, of a power greater than my own ego. That autonomous power I call God."

Surprisingly, irrationally, terrifyingly—without our knowing or willing it—that autonomous power works on each of us through our complexes.

For example, a young girl has been saddled with an inferiority complex due to the particular family constellation she was born into: an alcoholic father with whom she shared a similar feeling temperament, and a mother who devalued the feeling function, her husband and, by extension, her daughter. It became the daughter's unconscious conviction that she was stupid, unattractive and unlovable. The events of her youth seemed to confirm her mother's opinion which without realizing it she had adopted. (This is the self-fulfilling prophecy.) Her mother expected her to do poorly in school and she obliged. She got into relationships with men who were either unavailable or who degraded her as her family had. In her late thirties, defying nearly overwhelming fear and despair, she

---

[30] "Face to Face" interview by John Freeman, in *C.G. Jung Speaking,* p. 428.

returned to school and was surprised to discover she was a straight-A student.

We are usually unaware of our highest value, but whatever it is, that is our God. Often our highest value coincides with a complex that dictates how we perceive the world. This is what we live for and sacrifice everything for, including our happiness and the happiness of our children and spouse, without being aware of it. It is the task of depth psychotherapy to bring to consciousness the false God of our childhood complex so that the authentic God of our childhood Self can be given its rightful place.

Here are three descriptions that Jung has left us about his experience of the God-image:

God is Reality itself.[31]

God [is] that which stands up to [man] and determines his destiny.[32]

[God] is the name by which I designate all things that cross my willful path, violently and recklessly, all things that upset my subjective views, plans and intentions and change the course of my life for better or for worse.[33]

God is whatever defines a person's reality. That is the psychological meaning of God as Creator—God creates your reality. Whatever structures your world or orients you in it is the God you worship, knowingly or unknowingly.

Just as a truly religious person never questions whether his God exists, most people never realize that their perception of the world is something they unconsciously impose upon it. This error reveals itself most clearly in psychotherapy, where we learn that our assumptions about ourselves and the world may not correspond to "objective" reality. We must unlearn the version of the world we learned in childhood in order to be able to shed our illusions and

---

[31] "Answer to Job," *Psychology and Religion,* CW 11, par. 631.
[32] *Letters,* vol. 2, p. 66.
[33] Ibid., p. 525.

realize our destiny. Our neurotic version of the world corresponds to a false god.

This was not always so. In former times the childhood version of the world could remain useful throughout life. Life spans were shorter then and the world was not mutating at the exponential rate it is today. Only increased consciousness will enable us to function productively in this rapidly changing world.

It is not that childhood was any less traumatic in the past than today, only that certain factors compensated for the failings of the parents: the extended family, the community and a living religion. These three factors operating together, and dependent on one another, made a reality of the holy words, "When my father and my mother forsake me then the Lord will take me up."[34]

I think it is hard for us to imagine life in a religious time such as the Middle Ages when, psychologically, humans resembled fish sustained and nourished by the sea but unaware of what sustained them. We have nothing similar today. This is a tragic loss of which we are not even conscious.

There also exists a nonneurotic, consensual version of the everyday world. I mean categories like life and death and good and bad, which we forget are human categories. Colors and objects, smells and sounds, height and width and depth, the passage of time, none are given by nature but are imposed upon her by our subjectivity, the structure of our psyche. But because our subjectivity and outer reality partake of the same substance (both are "nature") there is of course a correspondence between them.

This becomes evident in the case of mathematics where human beings have elaborated a system: a product purely of the mind, only to discover subsequently that it has precise correspondences with outer reality, enabling us to predict, for example, the exact moment of an eclipse.

The point is that our minds impose structure upon the world and

---

[34] Ps. 27:10.

we are not aware of it. Whatever constructs our reality is our God. These God-images often take on a fourfold structure called a quaternity. The quaternity we know as space-time, for example, is composed of the three dimensions of length, width and depth, plus the fourth dimension, time. Alternatively the space-time quaternity can be considered to be past, present and future plus space.

The basic idea is that our mind has a need to order the world, and the mechanism of this ordering or structuring impulse seems to take the form of quaternities—somewhat like the cross-hairs in a telescope. The relationship to mandalas such as the Christian cross is evident. For example, if we are Christians and see the world with the cross imposed against it, as it were, it gives us our bearings.

Thus we are enabled to understand the reason for Jung's extended researches into the history and symbolism of mandalas and quaternities. They are representations of how we see reality or, in other words, how the psyche is ordered; in short, they are God-images. Put another way: a knowledge of quaternities exposes the underlying structure by which our minds operate, a mechanism otherwise unconscious to us.

In psychotherapy we deal with the lesser and the false gods: the complexes, personal myths, assumptions and illusions about the world which are imprinted upon us early in childhood and order our perceptions like gods or the space-time quaternity. These complexes, once constellated, are uncommonly stable and resistant to modification.

The figure on the next page illustrates how one's perceptions seem self-evident and may not be easily subject to change. What do *you* see—a young woman in three-quarter view with her head almost completely turned to her right, or an old crone, chin on chest, facing to the left (in the picture) and forward? Whichever image you may immediately register, you may or may not also be able to see the other. Both images are objectively present. The only variation is in the individual's perception.

Returning to the Jung passage at the beginning of this chapter,

one who is in touch with "the living presence of the eternal images" has access to God, that is, retains a connection to a particular template of God, and thus possesses an inner compass which guides him or her through the profusion of voices and choices. Jung is saying that a relationship to something greater than one's own ego bestows upon the psyche a dignity which makes it possible for the person to "stand by his own soul," that is, to maintain one's personal integrity against the onslaught of collective pressures.

*

Only then will he realize that the conflict is *in him,* that the discord and tribulation are his riches, which should not be squandered by attacking others; and that, if fate should exact a debt from him in the form of guilt, it is a debt to himself.

When a person can stand by his or her own soul (grant it highest value), one may then realize that problems, defeats and humiliations, though they seem to derive from sources outside oneself, are actually inside, and if understood as such have the potential to enrich life. But this can happen only if the inner life, the soul, is perceived to be of equal value to the outer world.

Jung offers the example of guilt. Many talk about guilt as if others have instilled it in them. But guilt has its deepest root in the limitations of the ego in comparison to the unlimited extent of the Self. Both the world of the soul and the outer world we call "reality" are of infinite extension and complexity, and we can do justice to only a small part of either. Something inner or outer is always being shortchanged. Therein lies our deepest source of guilt. We need to remember that in order for that conflict Jung is talking about (guilt) to be present, the higher power (God) must likewise be present. No one in whom God is not working feels guilty.

Conversely, an inability to feel guilt is commonly found in psychopaths. In such persons it is as if the God-image has become so obscured that nothing exists within them that could balance the claim of their egos to sovereignty. Because there is nothing sacred to the psychopath, that is, nothing more important than his or her own ego, there is nothing inside or outside that ego-demands can run up against—hence, no guilt. The psychopath may bump up against the claims of other people or of the state, but the psychopath's problem is only how to manipulate them. It is a conflict, to be sure, but not an inner conflict, thus no guilt is engendered.

The idea of guilt coming into the world at the same instant as consciousness is illustrated by the Adam and Eve story. Adam hides from God only after he has eaten of the Tree of Knowledge of Good and Evil, that is, become aware of the opposites. He knows now that he is different from Eve (and he therefore covers himself), and that he is different too from God. The same is true of Eve. They hide themselves because their newborn human will has instantly fallen into conflict with God's will. This conflict between their egos and the will of God represents the source of their guilt in that first instant of their birth as conscious beings and ever since. Perhaps it is also the source of the idea of original sin, the notion that consciousness per se implies guilt because it separates us from God.

The Western myth of consciousness is stated quite baldly in the Creation story of Adam and Eve. Though presumably content with their life in Paradise, their serpent nature one day got the better of them. In disobedience to the ordinance of God, the first couple found themselves stealing a taste of the fruit of the Tree of Knowledge of Good and Evil.

To recapitulate: guilt came into the world when Adam and Eve ate of the Tree of Knowledge (thus becoming conscious) and were confronted by God. Only with consciousness did God make his appearance. Previously, Adam and Eve were like fish in the sea: sustained by God (as fish are sustained by the waters) but unaware of God's presence.

The myth of Adam and Eve suggests that God is ambivalent about Adam's sin, since His omniscience would surely have permitted Him to thwart the will of Adam and Eve had He been undivided about it. Our Western creation myth suggests that the opposites are of God, and the ego (the center of consciousness) is the mirror in which, as Jung says, "the unconscious becomes aware of its own face."[35]

*

If the projected conflict is to be healed, it must return into the psyche of the individual, where it had its unconscious beginnings.

As long as one remains in thrall to the overwhelming power of the outer world, one will attempt to solve the inner conflict in the outer world. Only if the inner world is granted equal value will it be possible to transform the projected conflict.

Suppose, for example, a woman is emotionally abused as a child. Her mother is self-involved and unempathic to the extent that the child's feelings, thoughts and wishes do not exist. The child's demands are ruthlessly stamped out because to the narcissistic mother only such things have a right to exist in the child that the mother put there, or at any rate *expected* to find there.

Suppose, then, that this adult child of a narcissistic mother has minor surgery. She is kept waiting at the hospital two hours beyond her appointment time—two hours of nervousness, lightheadedness and discomfort because she has been forbidden to eat or drink since midnight the previous day. After the surgery, in the recovery room,

---

[35] *Mysterium Coniunctionis,* CW 14, par. 129.

she finds the nurses inattentive. She is angry and underneath the anger she is feeling hurt, helpless and hopeless, just as she did as a child. She wants to lash out, which is an understandable reaction. Though it may discharge tension, however, it will not promote psychic healing. Though somewhat mistreated in the hospital, the real injury was done to her as a child and that is what she is reexperiencing. If she can come to accept that fact, locating her current suffering in childhood where it first began, there may in time be born in her a "greater personality" (the Self) which is capable of understanding and soothing her in a way her parents never could.

*

He must celebrate a Last Supper with himself, and eat his own flesh and drink his own blood.

Drinking one's own blood means assimilating one's own affects (feelings, moods, emotions). Just as the Last Supper, celebrated as the Mass, became a central rite of Christianity, so in our present age the eating of one's own flesh and drinking of one's own blood is destined to become a central rite of the new religion. This rite is known as depth psychotherapy. The assimilation of one's affects, and attention to our inner wounded child, become a modern means of worship of and service to God or—the same thing—pathways toward individuation.

*

Is this perhaps the meaning of Christ's teaching, that each must bear his own cross?

Our cross is often the childhood complex which determined our outlook. A heavy burden. Or the cross can be the shadow, the inferiorities which each of us bears.

*

For if you have to endure yourself, how will you be able to rend others also?

This means that if you see your own shadow, you will not need to project it upon others. Jung writes:

> The shadow is a moral problem that challenges the whole ego-personality, for no one can become conscious of the shadow without considerable moral effort. To become conscious of it involves recognizing the dark aspects of the personality as present and real.[36]

Personally, I think of the shadow as the part of us that we don't want to be part of us.[37]

If you continue to celebrate a Last Supper with yourself, you will find yourself fully occupied with the nourishing and painful task of coming to terms with your personal reality. At the same time, other people's inferiorities—their complexes and shadows—will not affect you so much.

---

[36] "The Shadow," *Aion,* CW 9ii, par. 14.
[37] James Yandell, personal communication.

PART TWO
Practice

1
What Is Our Purpose in Life?

Whoso eateth my flesh, and drinketh my blood, hath eternal life.[38]

Psychologically understood, eternal life refers to the fact that a process such as depth psychotherapy has the power to grant us new life, that is, transform outmoded ways of being into new more fulfilling attitudes in keeping with our authentic nature.

For instance, small children have no defense against the intrusion of other people's (particularly their parents') complexes, hence they often take on a burdensome destiny projected upon them through the unconsciousness of others. Unwittingly, unconsciously, we take on our parents' myth, a myth that may have little or nothing to do with our own authentic nature.

Psychotherapy enables us to return to the infant that God made and to the child we were meant to be—in other words, we reexperience the trauma of childhood in order to reclaim our authentic selves.

What is our purpose in life? To shed one veil. To reveal a mystery. To illuminate in ourselves an aspect of God never before revealed. Every person's life, indeed every action, expresses a hidden truth. And this hidden truth illuminates an aspect of God. This is no more than saying, perhaps, that we were formed in the image of God. Or that our every word and deed is an expression of the Self. But this only happens if someone recognizes it. Otherwise our truth remains shrouded both to ourselves and our community.

This doesn't mean that every action must be public. But in order for our charitableness and generosity, for instance, to be transfor-

---

[38] John 6:54.

mative to *ourselves,* someone, at some time, must recognize us as a good and generous person. This will allow us to experience ourselves as such and this can be transformative.

Understanding and recognition is achieved in depth psychotherapy mainly through interpretation, the basic intervention of psychoanalysis. Many interpretations are made on the level of the personal unconscious, with current thoughts and actions and symptoms being related back to childhood experiences.

Interpretation grants meaning to experience and permits split-off elements of the psyche to be reconnected to the ego. Or, to put it another way: the ego, by paying devoted attention to the trauma (the source of the wounding), soothes the inner wounded child—the part of the psyche which is crying out for attention.

As the veils of illusion, the complexes, are dissolved, an aspect of God is illuminated. With the help of interpretation one sees oneself not "through a glass, darkly," but "face to face."[39] Most importantly, our childhood suffering is witnessed compassionately. At that moment it becomes real and the healing begins.

According to the Judeo-Christian myth as well as the Jungian myth, if a man or a woman is able to live out of his or her authentic being, a permanent deposit will be laid down in the collective psyche, a permanent contribution toward the evolution and differentiation of the God-image. This permanent deposit, this little star, the by-product of our struggle for consciousness, is equivalent to eternal life.

---

[39] 1 Cor. 13:12.

2

The Hymn of the Pearl

This Gnostic tale is a dramatic evocation of the functioning of the ego-Self axis, or the relation between man and God.

When I was a little child and dwelt in the kingdom of my Father's house and delighted in the wealth and splendor of those who raised me, my parents sent me forth from the East, our homeland, with provisions for the journey. . . . They took off from me the robe of glory which in their love they had made for me, and my purple mantle that was woven to conform exactly to my figure, and made a covenant with me, and wrote it in my heart that I might not forget it: "When thou goest down into Egypt and bringest back the One Pearl which lies in the middle of the sea which is encircled by the snorting serpent, thou shalt put on again thy robe of glory and thy mantle over it and with thy brother, our next in rank, be heir to our kingdom."

I left the East and took my way downwards, accompanied by two royal envoys, since the way was dangerous and hard and I was young for such a journey. . . . I went down into Egypt, and my companions parted from me. I went straightway to the serpent and settled down close by his inn until he should slumber and sleep so that I might take the Pearl from him. . . . I was a stranger to my fellow-dwellers in the inn. . . . I clothed myself in their garments, lest they suspect me as one coming from without to take the Pearl and arouse the serpent against me. But through some cause they marked that I was not their countryman, and they ingratiated themselves with me and mixed me drink with their cunning, and gave me to taste of their meat; and I forgot that I was the child of a king and served *their* king. I forgot the Pearl for which my parents had sent me. Through the heaviness of their nourishment I sank into deep slumber.

All this that befell me, my parents marked, and they were grieved for me. . . . And they wrote a letter to me, and each of the great ones signed it with his name.

"From thy father the King of Kings, and from thy mother, mistress of the East, and from thy brother, our next in rank, unto thee our child in Egypt, greeting. Awake and rise up out of thy sleep, and perceive the words of our letter. Remember that thou art the child of a king—yet behold whom thou has served in bondage. Be mindful of the Pearl, for whose sake thou has departed into Egypt. Remember thy robe of glory, recall thy splendid mantle, that thou mayest put them on and deck thyself with them and thy name be read in the book of the heroes and then become with thy brother, our deputy, heir to our kingdom."

Like a messenger was the letter. . . . It rose up in the form of an eagle, the king of all winged fowl and flew until it alighted beside me and became wholly speech. At its voice and sound I awoke and arose from my sleep, took it up, kissed it, broke its seal, and read.

Just as if it were written on my heart were the words of my letter to read. I remembered that I was a child of kings, and that my freeborn soul desired its own kind. I remembered the Pearl for which I had been sent down to Egypt, and I began to enchant the terrible and snorting serpent. I charmed it to sleep by naming over it my Father's name, the name of our next in rank, and that of my mother, the Queen of the East. I seized the Pearl, and turned to repair home to my Father. Their filthy and impure garment I put off, and left it behind in their land, and directed my way that I might come to the light of our homeland, the East.

My letter which had awakened me I found before me on my way; and just as it had awakened me with its voice so it guided me with its light that shone before me, and with its voice it encouraged me in my fear, and with its love it drew me on. . . .

[Then, as he approached his homeland, his parents sent out to him his robe of glory and his mantle.] And I stretched toward it and took it and decked myself with the beauty of its colors. And I cast the royal mantle about my entire self. Clothed therein, I ascended to the gate of salutation and adoration. I bowed my head and adored the splendor of my Father who had sent it to me, whose commands I had fulfilled as he too had done what he promised. . . . He received me joyfully, and I was with him in his kingdom.[40]

That is a poetic depiction of our life's journey from a spiritual point of view.

---

[40] Hans Jonas, *The Gnostic Religion*, pp. 113ff. (slightly modified).

The little child represents the ego which, though it has an original unconscious connection to God, tends to lose that connection in the course of its sojourn in Egypt. Egypt represents the material world into which we must descend in order to find the One Pearl, that is, individuate.

Our purpose on earth is to snatch back from the dragon the One Pearl, which means to discover the one we were meant to be.

From time to time we will receive a letter which reminds us of our purpose. The "letter" can be in the form of a message from the unconscious through a dream, fantasy, symptom, synchronistic event, or any other experience. That letter will remind us that we are the child of kings and that the garment of worldliness which we have put on does not reflect our complete nature. As it says, "Remember that thou art the child of a king. . . . Be mindful of the Pearl, for whose sake thou has departed into Egypt."

These injunctions convey the moral of the story—remember where you have come from and where you are going. To understand these important matters and to mature as individuals, we need more than mechanistic science, which can only inform us that we come from zygotes and end in the grave where we are reduced to our component chemicals.

Egypt symbolizes that realm of the ego which can hypnotize us and make us forget our purpose. Remembering our royal origins and our lofty goal may give us the energy and fortitude to challenge the serpent, who represents the dark powers—including fear, inertia, anger, greed, envy, gluttony and concupiscence. In the new religion, these must not be suppressed or repressed (as in traditional Christianity), but consciously related to.

That is what the new religion demands of us: that all of God's qualities which He has implanted in us should be consciously lived through—though not necessarily lived out.

3
Breaking the Chain of Suffering

The enlightened human consciousness breaks the chain of suffering
and thereby acquires a metaphysical and cosmic significance.[41]

Chain of suffering refers to the Buddhist idea of the causal linking
of desire, birth, sickness, suffering, old age and death.

Psychologically it can also be understood as referring to the
seemingly automatic repetition of patterns of belief, behavior and
thought (complexes) which we inherit from our family and unconsciously pass on to our children, for better or worse.

I think people in depth psychotherapy who undergo the pain of
reexperiencing their childhood woundings should be recognized as
heroes and rewarded with medals. Although most are rewarded
with a lightening of their burden and the disclosure of previously
unknown vistas, and while the human connection with the therapist
is often experienced as a comfort, the process of depth psychotherapy often feels like it contains a lot of unredeemed suffering.

Jung's words offer us meaning for our otherwise meaningless
suffering; both the suffering in childhood and the later suffering as
an adult are caused by the persistence of our defenses to intolerable
conditions in childhood. These defenses (such as anger or submis-
siveness) helped us survive then, but in adulthood, paradoxically,
they provoke the very situations they once protected us from. For
instance, the childhood expectation of being treated unkindly
(which expectation may have been quite warranted) evokes unsym-
pathetic responses in adulthood.

Those defenses (complexes), which our psyches automatically

---

[41] Jung, *Letters*, vol. 2, p. 311 (modified).

throw up in response to anything resembling the childhood trauma, perpetuate the chain of suffering that Jung speaks of.

In purely selfish terms, it may often be a question of whether the whole process of depth psychotherapy is worth it. This is where Jung comes in. He tells us that the quest to know ourselves, which may sometimes seem so narcissistic, has transpersonal consequences; that is to say, it affects other people, living, dead and yet unborn, and it affects God, the whole unconscious background of the cosmos.

Through our consciousness we redeem the suffering of those close to us, especially our children. Even if we can't escape entirely from the clutches of our complexes, a deep knowledge (not just intellectual) of our neuroses and the reexperiencing of our childhood wounds can release our loved ones from the necessity of inflicting upon others the wounds we inflicted upon them. That is how the chain of suffering is broken.

4
The Golden Rule and the Iron Rule

Do unto others as you would have them do unto you.[42]

This is the well-known golden rule, the ideal. But the *iron* rule, the operative rule, is, "You will do unto others as was done unto you." Becoming aware of a tendency somewhere within us to act according to the iron rule, many of us try to do just the opposite.

I know a woman I will call Julie. Her mother was one of those women whose role as mother was somewhat unsuitable and unfulfilling for her. Nevertheless Julie's mother had five children whose physical needs she took good care of but with whom she was self-centered, angry, critical, unempathic and emotionally neglectful. Julie then tried to give *her* child the loving attention she had missed. She neglected herself (just as her mother had neglected her) and her anger (to her great mortification) would leap out at her child, who reacted against being smothered and intruded upon by too much attention, which more appropriately should have been directed at Julie's own inner child.

If we wish to be healed and to break the chain of suffering, we have no choice but to reexperience our childhood trauma and stay in touch with that inner wounded child. The devotions in this book are meant to assist in that process.

---

[42] As in Matt. 7:12; Luke 6:31.

5

The Wounded Inner Child in the Bible

I want to take up a very famous text from the Hebrew Bible, the "suffering servant" passage from Isaiah, chapter 53. This passage was interpreted by Christians to refer to Jesus, thus forming a bridge between the Hebrew and Christian dispensations.

Psychologically understood, as referring to our wounded inner child, it can also be interpreted as forming a bridge that unites all three eras: Hebrew, Christian and Psychological.

He grew up before the Lord as a tender plant, and like a root out of dry ground; he had no form nor comeliness that we should look at him, and no beauty that we should desire him. He was despised and rejected by men; a man of sorrows, and acquainted with grief; we hid as it were our faces from him; he was despised, and we esteemed him not.

Surely he has borne our griefs and carried our sorrows; yet we esteemed him stricken, smitten by God, and afflicted. But he was wounded for our transgressions, he was bruised for our iniquities; upon him was the chastisement that made us whole, and with his stripes we are healed. . . . He was oppressed, and he was afflicted, yet he opened not his mouth; he was brought as a lamb to the slaughter, and as a sheep before her shearers is dumb, so he opened not his mouth. By oppression and judgment he was taken away; and who gave a thought to his fate: that he was cut off from the land of the living, stricken for the transgression of my people? And they made his grave with the wicked, and with the rich in his death, although he had done no violence, and there was no deceit in his mouth.

Yet it pleased the Lord to bruise him; he has put him to grief; when he makes himself an offering for sin, he shall see his offspring, he shall prolong his days; the will of the Lord shall prosper in his hand; he shall see the fruit of the travail of his soul and be satisfied; by his knowledge shall my righteous servant justify many; for he shall bear their iniquities.

Therefore will I divide him a portion with the great, and he shall divide the spoil with the strong; because he poured out his soul unto death, and he was numbered with the transgressors; yet he bore the sin of many, and made intercession for the transgressors.[43]

That is a poetic description of how and why we dissociate from our wounded inner child and how essential it is to recognize the value of our inner child. Although the inner child represents our wounded and afflicted self, to pay attention to her or him is painful, seemingly unprofitable and a distraction from worldly concerns (ego purposes). Our impulse is to distance ourselves from that child, as we would from bad luck or something accursed.

In the second paragraph we read:

Upon him was the chastisement that made us whole, and with his stripes we are healed.

This informs us that our wholeness is identified with our inner wounds and that we cannot rely on a firm sense of self so long as we dissociate from them. If we can reconnect with the pain of the wounded child, however, we may experience healing.

Isaiah's words agree with the experience of psychotherapists. If an adult can reexperience the childhood trauma in a secure setting this has a healing effect. Intellectual awareness alone is insufficient.

Thus far we have been interpreting this passage on the subjective level, that is, as it refers to the relationship between our ego and our inner child. It can also be understood on the objective level, as referring to the childhood relationship between our parents and ourselves. The suffering servant, oneself as a child, may have been misjudged, misunderstood and undervalued. We were made to feel bad, unworthy, flawed, unlovable, damaged goods—not what our parents wanted or expected—certainly not what they deserved. This made us feel ugly within, which in time transmuted itself into a (largely unconscious) negative self-image. To the extent that *any*

---

[43] Isa. 53:2-12, Revised Standard Version (slightly modified).

attitude remains unconscious it resists modification by reason. Only the reexperiencing of the original trauma is capable of modifying it.

In the fourth paragraph the key phrase is "when he makes himself an offering for sin," which means that if we stay in touch with our wounded child we will be granted new life. This statement is borne out by clinical experience. But if the suffering servant is guiltless (as the Biblical passage makes clear), one begins to wonder, "Whose sin is the suffering servant atoning for?" If there is anything that could be spoken of as sin, does it not lie with the Lord, perpetrator of this torment of the lamb?

Centuries later Isaiah's prophetic glimpse into the background of the psyche emerged into collective consciousness with the story of Job who, though guiltless, was nearly crushed by a suspicious God when He permitted Satan (an aspect of Himself) to try Job's faithfulness by calling down upon him a series of catastrophes beginning with the death of his children.

6

The Lesson of Job

Though he slay me, yet will I trust in him: but I will maintain mine own ways before him.[44]

Although Job's "comforters" were certain he was guilty of some unacknowledged sin that required atonement, Job, like Jacob before him, remained true to his own experience, insisting on continuing the dialogue with God until he obtained satisfaction.

Job's self-awareness, together with his love and trust in God, permitted him to demand justice from God. In return for his devotion, courage and self-knowledge, God answered Job out of the whirlwind and revealed something about himself that had not previously been known—that He is a phenomenon and not a man.

Job wonders why God treats him throughout as if he were an equal, "Wilt thou frighten a driven leaf and pursue dry chaff?"[45] Jung notes, "Job is challenged as though he himself were a god."[46] Apparently Job's consciousness had attained godlike proportions.

God makes it clear in the end that he favors the remonstrations of Job (to whom He restored prosperity) over the pious rationalizations of Job's comforters (whom He threatened for speaking untruthfully of Him).

According to the Jungian myth God seeks his unity through humankind.[47] Thus, individuation can be understood as the process by which the God-image differentiates and evolves.

---

[44] Job 13:15.
[45] Job 13:25, Revised Standard Version.
[46] "Answer to Job," *Psychology and Religion,* CW 11, par. 594.
[47] See Jung, *Letters,* vol. 2, p. 28; also Edward F. Edinger, *Transformation of the God-Image: An Elucidation of Jung's* Answer to Job, p. 15.

7
The Meaning of Suffering

Job is no more than the outward occasion for an inward process of dialectic in God.[48]

The naive assumption that the creator of the world is a conscious being must be regarded as a disastrous prejudice which later gave rise to the most incredible dislocations of logic.[49]

The idea that God has something to learn from man is hard for the modern mind to grasp, probably because of the "disastrous prejudice" that God is a conscious being. The emotional necessity for that notion is the relatively childlike state of our collective consciousness which requires the presence of a good parent on high. The idea that our parent is a mixture of opposites is difficult to swallow and it remains the most formidable stumbling-block to comprehension of the Jungian myth of the transformation of the God-image.

It may be that only those who have had the Job experience, who have seen the "back of Yahweh," the "abysmal world of shards"[50] —that is to say, those who have been first shattered and then healed by God—are in a position to reconcile the paradoxical God-image, what Jung called "God's tragic contradictoriness."[51]

The Jungian viewpoint complements the Freudian viewpoint just where the latter is weakest. Let me illustrate. The distinguished psychoanalyst Salman Akhtar was once asked a question which, I

---

[48] "Answer to Job," *Psychology and Religion*, CW 11, par. 587; also Edinger, *Creation of Consciousness*, p. 70.
[49] Ibid., par. 600, n. 13.
[50] Ibid., par. 595.
[51] *Memories, Dreams, Reflections*, p. 216.

imagine, was difficult for him to answer but which a Jungian would have less trouble with. The question was, what would be the optimal result of the psychoanalysis of a severe personality disorder? Akhtar responded with what he called a "parable" of two flower vases, both precious and of equal value, one shattered then restored by a master craftsman. He concludes:

> The lines along which [the shattered vase] had broken . . . will always remain discernible to an experienced eye. However, it will have a certain wisdom since it knows something that the vase that has never been broken does not: it knows what it is to break and what it is to come together.[52]

The Jungian myth can be considered an exploration of the *meaning* of being shattered or crushed. For many of us to whom this has occurred, this meaning is redemptive. It is important for us to know we were not shattered because of any inferiority, but because God apparently requires broken vessels. The Talmud tells us that human beings despise broken vessels but God loves them. Jung agrees:

> Because of his littleness, puniness, and defenselessness against the Almighty, [man] possesses . . . a somewhat keener consciousness based on self-reflection.[53]

There is no more effective goad to self-reflection than suffering.

---

[52] Review of *Broken Structures: Severe Personality Disorders and Their Treatment,* in "Psychotherapy Book News," vol. 26, October 15, 1992, p. 16.
[53] "Answer to Job," *Psychology and Religion,* CW 11, par. 579.

8
Holding the Opposites As Service to God

Olga Froebe-Kapteyn was the founder of the Eranos series of lectures at Ascona, Switzerland, which brought together scholars from throughout the world to discuss matters of spiritual moment. From 1933 to 1951 Jung was a frequent contributor.

Finding herself in the modern predicament of being split between motherhood and career, Froebe-Kapteyn sought Jung's advice in a letter which has not passed down to us. We have, however, Jung's reply:

> Your present situation is the result of pressure of circumstances which are unavoidable. It is *conflicts of duty* that make endurance and action so difficult. Your life's work for Eranos was unavoidable and right. Nevertheless it conflicts with maternal duties which are equally unavoidable and right. The one must exist, and so must the other. There can be no resolution, only patient endurance of the opposites which ultimately spring from your own nature. You yourself are a conflict that rages in itself and against itself, in order to melt its incompatible substances, the male and the female, in the fire of suffering, and thus create that fixed and unalterable form which is the goal of life. Everyone goes through this mill, consciously or unconsciously, voluntarily or forcibly. We are crucified between the opposites and delivered up to the torture until the "reconciling third" takes shape. Do not doubt the rightness of the two sides within you, and let whatever may happen, happen. Admit that your daughter is right in saying you are a bad mother, and defend your duty as a mother towards Eranos. But never forget that Eranos is also the right thing and was latent within you from the beginning. The apparently unendurable conflict is proof of the rightness of your life. A life without inner contradiction is either only half a life or else a life in the Beyond, which is destined only for angels. But God loves human beings more than the angels.[54]

---

[54] *Letters,* vol. 1, p. 375.

Let us consider Jung's views more closely.

It is *conflicts of duty* that make endurance and action so difficult.

Conflicts of duty are neither inexplicable nor due to the intervention of malevolent forces, but rather a reflection of our having been formed in the image of God who Himself (according to the Jungian myth) is a *complexio oppositorum* (a union of opposites). Our honest attempt to hold the opposites in awareness, according to the Jungian myth, contributes to the evolution and differentiation of the God-image.

*

There can be no resolution, only patient endurance of the opposites which ultimately spring from your own nature.

This sentence has often been a comfort to me. It contains two propositions: 1) solving the problem is not the point—our responsibility lies solely in holding in awareness the irreconcilable opposites; and 2) the suffering we endure in that process belongs to our nature and is therefore relevant to the individuation process.

*

You yourself are a conflict that rages in itself and against itself, in order to melt its incompatible substances, the male and the female, in the fire of suffering, and thus create that fixed and unalterable form which is the goal of life.

Paradoxically, perceiving myself as a conflict soothes me because it validates and lends meaning to my experience of being in conflict so much of the time. If I am a mixture of incompatible substances, it explains why life has been such a struggle.

Something "fixed and unalterable" reminds me of gold and of Jung's last reported dream.

He saw a great round stone in a high place, a barren square, and on it were engraved the words: "And this shall be a sign unto you of Wholeness and Oneness." Then he saw many vessels to the right in an open square and a quadrangle of trees whose roots reached around the earth and enveloped him, and among the roots golden threads were glittering.[55]

*

We are crucified between the opposites and delivered up to the torture until the "reconciling third" takes shape.

Jung now introduces another metaphor—crucifixion. If we are being crucified then our honest struggle to be aware of the opposites in ourselves resembles Christ's mission. The hoped-for compensation for the torture of holding the opposites in our mind is an unexpected "third" which reconciles the opposites in the manner of the third item in the sequence, thesis, antithesis, synthesis.

Christ, whom people have worshipped for two millennia, is within us, just as was foretold in the scriptures: "The kingdom of God is within you."[56] Our wounded inner child, "hated for no reason,"[57] is equivalent to none other than Christ. Therefore making the effort to care for that inner child corresponds to caring for the sick, hungry, imprisoned Christ.[58]

*

The apparently unendurable conflict is proof of the rightness of your life. A life without inner contradiction is either only half a life or else a life in the Beyond, which is destined only for angels. But God loves human beings more than the angels.

If we experience ourselves as crucified, that is, torn between the opposites (which are of our own nature), then we live a life resembling Christ's. In other words, we are individuating. God values human beings who experience evil as well as good within them-

---

[55] Recounted in Marie-Louise von Franz, *C.G. Jung: His Myth in Our Time,* p. 287.
[56] Luke 17:21.
[57] John 15: 25, Jerusalem Bible.
[58] See Matt. 25:31-46; also Jaffe, *Liberating the Heart: Spirituality and Jungian Psychology,* pp. 51f.

selves, more than perfection. God loves human beings more than the angels because human beings, in their determined attempts to resolve conflict and uncertainty, assist God in sorting out His own nature. It is human beings who have been formed in the image of God and express not only God's justice but His "tragic contradictoriness."

9
Wrestling with the Angel

And Jacob was left alone; and there wrestled a man with him until the breaking of the day.

And when [the man] saw that he prevailed not against him, he touched the hollow of his thigh; and the hollow of Jacob's thigh was out of joint, as he wrestled with him.

And [the man] said, Let me go, for the day breaketh. And [Jacob] said, I will not let thee go, except thou bless me.[59]

The Bible tells us that on the day of this dream Jacob's father-in-law Laban, with his men, had overtaken a fleeing Jacob and threatened to strip him of his wives Leah and Rachel, his children and his flocks—the savings of twenty years of service to Laban. Jacob successfully concluded an agreement with Laban but the following day his brother Esau (whose birthright Jacob had stolen) was arriving with four hundred men. Jacob knew this encounter could cost him his life.

The man who assaults Jacob in the middle of the night identifies himself as an angel or messenger of God. Psychologically he represents Jacob's emotion, which he must come to terms with if he is to survive the next day's meeting with a wronged elder brother of superior strength. Jacob wrestles the whole night long with his anger and fear and this prepares him for his trial the following day. He not only declines to flee from his inner adversary, but insists on a blessing before releasing his more powerful foe.

With his outer adversary Esau, by contrast, Jacob adopts a conciliatory attitude, bowing humbly and lavishing him with gifts. This strategy succeeds in gaining Esau's favor.

---

[59] Gen. 32:24-26.

Jacob's courage and heroism in the inner world cultivates an attitude which promotes success in the outer world. The thoughts and images that disturb our sleep are meaningful messengers of God, not random phenomena to be quelled with pills.

The attitude epitomized by Jacob's words, "I will not let thee go, except thou bless me," is often evidenced by patients whose God-given courage enables them to hold their troubles in consciousness until such time as their meaning is revealed. This process has a transformative effect.

The angel of God grants Jacob a new name, Israel, which means in Hebrew, "He struggles with God." Through his honest struggle with the trouble that seized him in the night (when he was trying to rest in preparation for his ordeal the following day), Jacob has become a new man, in that a new name represents a new identity.

Jacob's new name became the name for a whole people whom he fathered. Interestingly, the Jews are called not the Children of Abraham, the Children of Isaac or the Children of Moses but the Children of Israel.[60] This suggests that, like their father Jacob, the Jews are in their essence identified with the process of transformation, the depth psychological name of which is individuation.

---

[60] Levi Meier, *Jewish Values in Jungian Psychology*, p. 124.

10
The Redemptive Value of Consciousness

All things are in the hand of the Lord except the fear of the Lord.[61]

Heredity and early environment, the factors which largely determine our character, are beyond our control. As the fish is ignorant of the great sea that sustains it, we are likewise unconscious of the culture which supports us, and we lack, at least in childhood, an objective standpoint which would enable us to evaluate it.

Our fate is decided in the first five or six years of life (as Freud discovered) except for one small but indispensable element (as Jung discovered). Our text calls this element, "the fear of the Lord," which, psychologically interpreted, corresponds to consciousness. Everything that happens to us is in the hands of the Lord except for one thing—our consciousness of it, and on that one thing a world depends.

It is only a slight exaggeration to say that by the time we get old enough to realize what's happened to us, everything we most fear and hate has already taken place. The only question which remains, is to what extent will those childhood events (which we have been calling complexes) continue to determine our lives.

The answer to that question is in our hands. It requires immense courage (in medieval terms, love and fear of God) to carry on with our struggle to be as conscious as possible, but that struggle is our rite of worship in the new religion. We have it in our power to continue until death our determination to acknowledge the truth even if it is very painful. The spirit of truth is another name for the Holy

---

[61] Kabbalistic legend, quoted in Gerhard Adler, *Studies in Analytical Psychology,* p. 120.

Spirit, one of the manifestations of God.

It is terrifying to witness the irreparable injury done to children, not intentionally, but through the unconsciousness of their parents. Then the children, when grown, treat *their* children as they were treated. And because all parents want what is best for their children, all of this occurs unwittingly, unconsciously. This cycle would be unendurable unless there were meaning in it. The meaning is provided by the Jungian understanding that consciousness is in itself redemptive, in that it serves God.

We cannot alter what happens to us, but we can alter our attitude toward what happens, which will change our experience. Why not then just make up our mind to change our attitude?

Unfortunately, mere conscious resolves are usually ineffectual. Moreover they constitute a kind of inflation because they impute God-like powers to human beings (creation of a new attitude). We are powerless to create new attitudes through an act of will. Only the religious attitude of careful consideration has the power to alter one's subjectivity in any profound and abiding way.

Jung says that man's destiny is "to create a cosmos from the chaotic mess into which one is born."[62] Certainly there is something in us that functions to make sense of our lives.

---

[62] *Letters,* vol. 2, p. 171.

11

"I Do Good Work"

I wondered for a long time how it was that all therapists, even ones about whom I had strong misgivings, thought they did "good work." An analysand of mine, for example, was seeking to affiliate himself with a group practice. From his interview with them he came away with doubts about their maturity, competence—even their integrity. Nevertheless, he reported that they were certain they did good work. He wishes he could have such confidence in himself. On the other hand he admits to feeling that he himself does good work.

When I think about it I recognize that I too feel I do good work. I realize I've heard that phrase frequently—every therapist I know does "good work."

Clearly therapeutic work varies in quality. For instance, I do better work now than I did thirty years ago, at which time I thought that my work was not just good but superb.

Therefore there must be something about the work of a therapist which convinces each of us that we are doing splendidly.

I think of my own analysts. I could say that each one (there were five) was just what I needed at the time. On the other hand I could envision the possibility (one in particular comes to mind) that another analyst could have served me better.

What then of the illusion (if that was what it was) that each of my analysts was just what I needed at the time? It reminds me of my life, of the important decisions I have made—vocation, marriage, etc.—and I wonder, "What if it had been different?" Yet what actually took place makes such supreme sense. Something in us seems to make a meaningful whole out of our experience. Indeed, man has been called the animal that produces meaning.

Take the sacrament of confession. It seems to be reasonably effective without regard to which priest is hearing the confession. Certainly every priest is justified in thinking that he, or God, does good work. Perhaps then it is God that is doing good work if He is but given half a chance. And each of us has a certain gift of healing. In some it is great, in others small. In some it works powerfully and purely, in others it is muted. In each it takes a different turn. But every psychotherapist, successful to any degree, is a healer.

No matter how the healing works or how large or small it is, it remains an impressive experience to those who share in it.

12
A New Form of Worship

Man's relation to God probably has to undergo a certain important change: Instead of the propitiating praise to an unpredictable king or the child's prayer to a loving father, the responsible living and fulfilling of the divine will in us will be our form of worship of and commerce with God.[63]

Understood psychologically, "the responsible living and fulfilling of the divine will in us" refers to the individuation process. In the psychological age attention to the unconscious becomes the equivalent of prayer.

According to the Jungian myth, God is now weary of empty praises just as he wearied earlier of human, then animal, sacrifices. Jung's hypothesis is that what God now requires is attention to His voice within—that our lives can become true expressions of His plan for us and that our lives (like Job's) can serve Him by flaring for a moment in the darkness that He has left still unnamed.

It took me into my sixties to understand the interminable praising of God that occupies such a central place in the prayers of Jews, Christians and Moslems. Then I realized that this is the way one would approach a testy and unpredictable tyrant (like the Old Testament Yahweh) who held one's life in his hands. By propitiating him one would hope to evoke his beneficent side.

This is not much different from the way human beings approach each other, especially when the other is someone in a superior position and has something to offer. It is the basis of good manners, gift giving, the display of an open hand and an open countenance. Trust, love, openness and gratitude are the traits most likely to evoke

---

[63] Jung, *Letters,* vol. 2, p. 316.

kindness and generosity and turn away angry retaliation, cruelty and vindictiveness. In the past both God and man have been capable of showing either side of their nature, the kind or the cruel.

I think that on our one small and beleaguered planet we are trying to learn to be kinder to one another, which suggests an evolution of the God-image in line with the incarnation in Jesus of God's loving side.

The idea that criminals are essentially abused children for whom no tear has been shed may be psychologically accurate, but it is hard to swallow for those of us still ruled by the law of talion ("an eye for an eye, a tooth for a tooth"). Offenders who remain unpunished and grinning at us from behind their typewriters or their lawyers can be infuriating to some of us. (More precisely, our inner criminals whom we have locked up begin rattling their cages demanding similar privileges.)

Perhaps we need to extend amnesty and a course of compassionate psychotherapy to our inner criminals. This, in any event, is what the new religion calls for. Jesus' doctrine of love and compassion, though unimplemented in the Christian age, has helped prepare the soil of our psyche for the new religion in which both God's loving and terrible sides are destined to be assimilated.

That need for vengeance in us and in God, the ancient talionic law, is destined to be mitigated in favor of understanding, compassion and forgiveness.

13
The Healing of Childhood Wounds

Before I formed you in the womb I knew you and before you were born I consecrated you.[64]

Only when someone catches a glimpse of us in our eternal essence can we sense who we really are, and begin to find a secure foundation for our lives.

It is one of the main tasks of psychotherapy to catch a glimpse of our essential nature, which previously had been hidden from ourselves. Just as we only see our shadow through relationship, we are dependent on another to first glimpse our essential goodness—the God within us. In India people greet each other with the word *Namaste*, which means, "I salute your spirit." I think this is what a good therapist offers, saluting the spirit of the patient—recognizing and showing respect for the invisible essence of the other.

Communicating to another one's deep understanding has been called *mirroring*. One example of mirroring is the gleam in the mother's eye, which reflects the God-like nature of her child. Another example would be carrying the person in one's mind: thinking about the other, anticipating his or her needs, being attuned to the other. The mirroring person perceives the dignity and infinite worth of the other's soul or destiny. This is not always, or even often, a conscious process.

When a person's Self or self-esteem or sense of dignity has been deeply injured, this is equivalent to an injury to the soul, to the God-image imprinted upon the psyche. This image of God, this soul whom God meant us to be, is of the highest value and is, in a

---

[64] Jer. 1:5, Revised Standard Version.

way, indestructible. This fact provides depth psychotherapy its rationale, for if one's self-image cannot be transformed, what then is the worth of all our labors? Thus Edinger describes the ultimate task of Jungian analysis as "the reconstruction of the God-image in the individual."[65]

On the other hand an injury to the soul often results in the wounded-god reaction, rage, an unleashing of the wrath of God.

It should be no surprise that we can react as if we were gods, because our likeness to God is clearly set forth in scripture: "God created human beings in his own image; in the image of God he created them."[66]

As Jung says, "We must read the Bible or we shall not understand psychology,"[67] and, "The statements made in the Holy Scriptures are also utterances of the soul."[68]

---

[65] *The Aion Lectures,* p. 94.
[66] Gen. 1:27, Revised English Bible.
[67] *The Visions Seminars,* p. 156.
[68] "Answer to Job," *Psychology and Religion,* CW 11, par. 557.

14

Success Versus Consciousness

These days I try to keep in mind two quotations:

Man's sacred mission is correction.[69]

The world is not *supposed* to work. All it does effectively is produce consciousness.[70]

These ideas help me to accept my errors or failures by reminding me that the purpose of life is not success—but consciousness.

It is frustrating to constantly strive for success because most of us have been saddled with childhood complexes which have distorted our view of life and ourselves. These distortions, together with the increasingly complex world in which we live, where no reliable principles exist to guide us through the mass of decisions each of us must make, can be depended upon to generate mistakes—often serious ones.

An animal lives in accordance with its instincts, which God has implanted; it never departs far from the will of God, or nature. A person fortunate enough to have been born into a viable culture (say medieval Christian Europe) lives according to the values and traditions of that culture and likewise seldom errs.

But if you are alienated from your culture because childhood events taught you to distrust it or because you sense its decadence, then your life must become a series of errors and attempts at correction. All that this process can yield, reliably, is consciousness, but if consciousness is your highest value you know that you serve God and that your life has meaning.

Near the end of his life, Jung put it like this:

---

[69] Talmudic saying.
[70] Robert Johnson, *The Double Animus,* audiotape.

Man's task is . . . to become conscious of the contents that press upward from the unconscious. Neither should he persist in his unconsciousness, nor remain identical with the unconscious elements of his being, thus evading his destiny, which is to create more and more consciousness. As far as we can discern, the sole purpose of human existence is to kindle a light in the darkness of mere being. It may even be assumed that just as the unconscious affects us, so the increase in our consciousness affects the unconscious.[71]

This is truly a radical statement, for boiled down to its essence it means nothing less than that the purpose of human life is the creation of consciousness.

---

[71] *Memories, Dreams, Reflections,* p. 326.

15
Jung on the Life of Christ

In October of 1937, Jung delivered the Terry Lectures at Yale University.[72] Later, at a gala dinner party to mark the end of his visit, Jung spoke off the cuff about the relation between his school of analytical psychology and religion. He ended with these words:

Jesus, you know, was a boy born of an unmarried mother. Such a boy is called illegitimate, and there is a prejudice which puts him at a great disadvantage. He suffers from a terrible feeling of inferiority for which he is certain to have to compensate. Hence the temptation of Jesus in the wilderness, in which the kingdom was offered to him. Here he met his worst enemy, the power devil; but he was able to see that, and to refuse. He said, "My kingdom is not of this world." But "kingdom" it was, all the same. And you remember that strange incident, the triumphal entry into Jerusalem. The utter failure came at the Crucifixion in the tragic words, "My God, my God, why hast thou forsaken me?" If you want to understand the full tragedy of those words you must realize what they meant: Christ saw that his whole life, devoted to the truth according to his best conviction, had been a terrible illusion. He had lived it to the full absolutely sincerely, he had made his honest experiment, but it was nevertheless a compensation. . . . But because he had lived so fully and devotedly he won through to the Resurrection body.

We must all do just what Christ did. We must make our experiment. We must make mistakes. We must live out our own vision of life. And there will be error. If you avoid error you do not live; in a sense even it may be said that every life is a mistake, for no one has found the truth. When we live like this we know Christ as a brother, and God indeed becomes man. This sounds like a terrible blasphemy, but not so. For then only can we understand Christ as he would want to be understood, as a fellow man; then only does God become man in ourselves.

---

[72] "Psychology and Religion," *Psychology and Religion,* CW 11.

This sounds like religion, but it is not. I am speaking just as a philosopher. People sometimes call me a religious leader. I am not that. I have no message, no mission; I attempt only to understand. We are philosophers in the old sense of the word, lovers of wisdom. That avoids the sometimes questionable company of those who offer a religion.

And so the last thing I would say to each of you, my friends, is: Carry through your life as well as you can, even if it is based on error, because life has to be undone, and one often gets to truth through error. Then, like Christ, you will have accomplished your experiment. So, be human, seek understanding, seek insight, and make your hypothesis, your philosophy of life. Then we may recognize the Spirit alive in the unconscious of every individual. Then we become brothers of Christ.[73]

In comparing our struggles with Christ's Jung offers a message of consolation. Serious errors in our life are unavoidable; in fact they are often the only way we can get to the truth about ourselves and about life. On the cross Christ realized that his whole life was in error—that it was a compensation for inferiority feelings evoked by his illegitimate birth, a circumstance much reviled in his day. The compensation was his conviction that he was the son of God, of highest worth. On the cross he realized that his whole life had been a compensation. The fact that his whole life was, in a way, an illusion was redeemed by the sincerity and devotion with which he conducted himself.

Christ's revelation on the cross of the truth about himself made possible the resurrection—psychologically, new life.

This image teaches us that if we see the truth about ourselves, even if it is in our last days, we redeem our children and our loved ones who had been affected by the illusion we lived in. In other words, we free them, retroactively, from the worst effects of the neurosis we inadvertently perpetrated upon them.

We all begin our lives in illusion, under the sway of our family

---

[73] *C.G. Jung Speaking*, pp. 97f.

myth or complex. To the degree that we achieve self-awareness during our lifetime, we gain distance from the complexes we inherited from our parents. Often it is only later in life that we begin to see our lives more clearly, shorn of the defenses against the unspeakable truths of our childhood situation.

This recognition has a negative and a positive aspect. On the negative side, it is tragic to have lived one's life under an illusion; on the positive side, our new awareness has a redemptive effect on both ourselves and our loved ones.

16
Studying Torah and Studying Jung

The Torah shall not depart from your lips and you shall meditate thereon day and night.[74]

These words have meant a lot to me because they have linked me back to generations of Jews poring over their Torahs just as I, a modern Jew, pore over Jung. Reading Jung reawakens me to a realm of meaning that I keep forgetting because I so readily get caught up in the little dramas of daily life. Studying Jung enables me to identify with my fathers who pored night and day over a holy text.

---

[74] Josh. 1:8, Anchor Bible.

17
Redemption Through Shadow Work

The shadow is the block which separates us most effectively from the divine voice.[75]

Work on the shadow represents the main content of most analyses. The shadow is the part of us that we don't want to be part of us. But if we succeed in carrying it in consciousness it is capable of transforming into something redemptive. This constitutes a frequent theme in myths and fairy tales *(The Frog Prince, Beauty and the Beast, King Arthur, Khundry,* etc.) It is also the main theme of the alchemical myth in which the process of transforming matter into gold begins with the *prima materia,* the first or most basic (and basest) material.

Jung taught us that the alchemical opus represented a projection of the unconscious onto matter. The alchemical effort to transmute base matter into gold foreshadowed our modern depth psychotherapeutic effort to transmute the shadow into the highest value, our hidden self. Thus the alchemical opus in our day has been converted into the psychoanalytic opus.

Psychotherapy focuses on the disturbing occurrences of everyday life. This process of concentrating attention taps feeling and emotion, which is to say it liberates heat so that the material under discussion goes through a series of changes and, *Deo concedente* (God willing), produces gold. But this only happens (the alchemists tell us and psychotherapists agree) if the vessel is tightly sealed, which is to say, when secure boundaries are in place, such as a regular neutral place and time for patient and therapist to meet free

---

[75] Jung, *Letters,* vol. 2, p. 545.

of interruptions. This is called the therapeutic container. If it is not secure the heat leaks out and the material doesn't cook—so psychic transformation fails to occur.

To be sure, it is often depressing to look at our shadow, but our chance for renewal lies to a great extent in accepting what we have rejected about ourselves. Moreover, the shadow also has a positive aspect: our unlived potential.

18

A Psychological View of the First Commandment

Thou shalt have no other gods before me.[76]

Complexes function like gods which nothing can move but a greater God. The Self (God) repudiates neuroses (other gods) because our complexes represent an obstacle to becoming in this world what God meant us to be. To allow ourselves to be ruled by our neuroses without challenging them is displeasing to God. The Talmud says, "Man's sacred mission is correction"; that is, we have a duty to confront our complexes and try to assimilate them through the application of consciousness. Put another way, our primary task in life is to accomplish God's purpose for us.

"Correction" is equivalent, psychologically, to the individuation process, an ongoing rediscovery of oneself. The situation into which we were born, which begins to dawn on us typically around age seven, is merely the departure point. We have the rest of our lives to correct the mistakes of our parents, to dismantle the childhood complexes (which were meant to defend the nascent Self against the error of our parents' ways) and discover who we were meant to be. Though our family may have misunderstood us, an invisible power exists that knows what we were meant to be and works to assist us in reclaiming our authentic nature.

According to the Jungian myth this process of correction serves the divine will. God functions in our psyche to organize our perceptions into a cross-hair or template. (This is why Jung was so interested in the symmetrical fourfold structures known as quaternities; he saw them as representations of the God-image.)

---

[76] Exod. 20:3.

79

The cross-hairs or templates we discovered in childhood and found redemptive (because they ordered our childhood reality in a way that enabled us to survive) have now outlived their usefulness and lie putrefying in the darkness of repression, poisoning the possibility of new life. Patients come to therapists in thrall to perceptions of reality which, while valid in childhood, now hamper their development, producing symptoms and forcing them to seek help.

Children take for granted the circumstances into which they were born. They have no objective standard by which to compare their family of origin, and though it may sometimes be terrifying and cruel it remains "home" to them. Besides they must deserve it (they think). Even in family situations injurious enough to require child protection agencies to intervene and place the children in a foster home, children typically blame themselves. Also if the parents are unhappy, children blame themselves. The thoughtful and conscientious parents of five-year old Jimmy had carefully planned how they would break the news of their divorce to him but Jimmy quickly got wind of what was coming and began crying, "I won't do it anymore!"

Although popular opinion holds that it is childish to blame others and more evolved to blame oneself, clinical experience suggests otherwise. Small children take their situation for granted just as a lamb goes to the slaughter. They don't blame their predicament on their parents because that would require a degree of emotional separation from their parents which they have not achieved. Their egos are not sufficiently developed to grant them perspective on their situations, nor do they have sufficient experience of the world to enable them to compare their situations with those of others. Many patients must be helped to see how crushed they were in childhood.

The child becomes convinced that he or she is bad or ugly or stupid, and this conviction becomes a deeply ingrained truth that is no longer questioned because "God" (in the person of the parents) has spoken. I am unlovable. That is my myth. That is my deepest belief, even if intellectually I don't believe anyone to be unlovable.

This myth of unlovableness becomes a template, an unconscious inner guiding principle that structures subsequent experience. As one who has been stamped with this template goes through life, it is as if the meaning (that one is bad or unlovable and should be rejected) is known beforehand and all that is in doubt are the circumstances which will demonstrate it. That myth or unconscious expectation exerts a powerful, invisible force on events and other people. If one feels ugly and worthy of rejection, people shy away.

It should be noted that the myth or complex derives much of its power from the fact that it is a uniting theory which bestows *meaning* upon experience. Meaning seems to be as essential as food to human existence. If my unlovableness becomes an unconscious uniting theory (complex) which orders experience for me, then it tends to repeat itself until a superior uniting theory displaces it. In the absence of psychotherapy this ordinarily doesn't happen.

It is the task of therapists to understand those templates or gods which their patients worship in the form of their childhood patterns of perception and behavior—otherwise called myths, complexes or neuroses. The therapist must first accept and understand and then must lead the analysand out of the Egypt of his or her outmoded beliefs to the promised land of their new, adult ways of being—to what they were meant to be when God formed them in the womb.

Patients don't realize it consciously (though they do unconsciously in the guise of symptoms, guilt or anxiety) but they are sinning in that they are violating the first commandment which states, "Thou shalt have no other gods before me." Thus *Reality* (which is how God defines himself in Exodus 3:14, *I am*) speaks, saying, "You must not let your neurosis (your mother's or father's myth), hinder your devotion to the one true God, *Reality Itself* (inner as well as outer)."

Translated into psychological language, the first commandment would read, "You must shed the childhood fog of neurosis in favor of the light of truth, your adult reality."

The templates or grids or cross-hairs laid down in childhood become the unconscious governing principles that can determine a person's whole life. They become habits of thinking and perception which have a surprising ability to shape *outer* events in the image of the person's *inner* reality or myth.

An example of this phenomenon, known as the self-fulfilling prophecy, was given above: the person who unconsciously feels unlovable. Because of the expectation of rejection, one doesn't notice the glimmerings of interest from others. Hence one is more likely to draw upon oneself the anticipated fate. This phenomenon has also been called the "repetition compulsion." It is as if the psyche wishes to repeat the trauma in order to resolve it. The psyche won't allow us to forget soul-murder; not until it has been healed on an inner level.

A straightforward example of the self-fulfilling prophecy is how the anticipation of a sleepless night can keep one awake. A good night's sleep is a gift of Mother Nature but if you didn't have a good-enough "night mother," fears and insecurities may mushroom under cover of darkness. In time the ego can learn to soothe the frightened and anxious child.

19
Testimony to the Holocaust

From a low hill in the Athi plains of East Africa I once watched the vast herds of wild animals grazing in soundless stillness, as they had done from time immemorial, touched only by the breath of a primeval world. I felt then as if I were the first man, the first creature, to know that all this *is*. The entire world round me was still in its primeval state; it did not know that it *was*. And then, in that one moment in which I came to know, the world sprang into being; without that moment it would never have been. All Nature seeks this goal and finds it fulfilled in man, but only in the most highly developed and most fully conscious man. Every advance, even the smallest, along this path of conscious realization adds that much to the world.[77]

To Jung's testimony to the value of consciousness I would like to append my own, which concerns the Holocaust. I have to declare at the outset that as a Jew born just at the time that Hitler came to power (though fortunately in America) I feel a special stake in the subject.

It was Jung's discovery of the transformative power of consciousness or witnessing that led me to the answer to a question which had long puzzled me: "What distinguishes the Holocaust from other massacres, mass murders and genocides?"

Many answers to this question have been offered but the one that satisfies me is based on the Jungian myth of the redemptive function of consciousness.

The answer, briefly stated, is this: prodded by the Jews, Western civilization has been obliged to hold *this* genocide in mind. In other

---

[77] "Psychological Aspects of the Mother Archetype," *The Archetypes and the Collective Unconscious,* CW 9i, par. 177.

words, the Holocaust, the most extensively recorded and best remembered of the atrocities that mar human history, is distinguished by the degree of consciousness accompanying it. Both the perpetrators and especially the victims of the "final solution" have extensively documented their testimony. Holocaust museums have opened in most Western nations and, a half-century after the event, the stream of written, oral, visual and artistic materials shows no sign of abating.

Many Jews claim that what happened to them is unique in human history. Perhaps, perhaps not, but the Jews are so passionately convinced of it that they succeed in keeping that vision of the unspeakable degradation of the human spirit before us. They insist, as their father Jacob did when he wrestled with the angel of God, "I will not let thee go, except thou bless me."[78] In other words, "I will not let this trouble depart from me until it yields up its meaning."

The meaning, according to Jung's hypothesis, is that consciousness is in itself redemptive. Applied to the present case: through contemplating the abomination of the Holocaust we increase our understanding of evil—how it develops (when we lose sight of the wounding), how it plays itself out (in mutual wounding) and how the seeds of a new cycle of evil are laid in the wounds.[79]

The Holocaust reveals a face of God and of human beings so terrifying and so remote from everyday notions of ourselves that a millennial process will be necessary to assimilate it. Today we are merely preparing the texts which will serve as the objects of contemplation for future generations. Meanwhile the process of assimilating the Holocaust goes on largely outside awareness.

We have already learned from the Holocaust more perhaps than we realize. The high valuation we place on tolerance and our efforts, insufficient though they may be, on behalf of the disabled, the

---

[78] See above, pp. 61f.
[79] See Myron B. Gubitz, "Amelek: The Eternal Adversary," in *Psychological Perspectives*, vol. 8, no. 1 (Spring 1977).

homeless, AIDS victims, the poor and minorities of every description are, in part, an unconscious compensation for the relative silence and inaction of both the temporal and "spiritual" authorities during the Holocaust. Today the main energies of many churches seem directed toward social justice.

Aiding the underdog now bestows meaning upon the lives of many. Worthy as this effort is, the new religion, the Psychological Dispensation we are now entering, requires a further step: the recognition that the lowliest underdog of all resides within us and cries out for attention. The ancient name for this inner underdog is the soul, but for modern people it is not discernible as an inner entity except as some are now encountering it in the form of the wounded inner child. Work on the inner child puts them in touch with something of infinite value *within* which is capable of counterbalancing the overwhelming power of the *outer* world, the collective. Thus we witness, in our day, a rebirth of the inner world (soul) in the guise of the abused child within us. The child archetype or image (e.g., the Christ-child) has always been a favorite form for God to assume when emerging into consciousness.

The wounded child is on the one hand abused and scapegoated, and on the other hand redemptive. It is the same archetype of the scapegoated and chosen one that the Jews have carried for humanity since they were called out of Egypt.

Returning now to a discussion of the Holocaust. The post-World War One Germans, humiliated by the Versailles peace treaty, unconsciously compensated by reaching out for the chosen or redemptive side of the scapegoat archetype and attempted to realize their ideals of purity, heroism and spirit. Perhaps predictably it was Germany, the most romantic yet the most rational and scientific of nations, the most advanced and civilized of peoples, who fell prey to the inflation that results from identification with any archetype. With fierce devotion they tested their mad hypothesis (that they could rid themselves of all darkness) and it was through them that the cancer of the Holocaust fulminated into human history. They showed us what rationality, divorced from feeling, can accomplish.

They penetrated into the background of the liberal, progressive, rationalistic ideas of the Enlightenment. To them, behind all of the codicils and the reasons, lay instinct and power—"Blood and Iron." Just as Freud saw through the pretensions and self-delusions of civilized life on the personal level, so the Germans, informed by the genius of Nietzsche, saw through the veneer of civilized life on the collective level. They carried a single idea through to its natural conclusion and did not fear to put it into action, the idea being: "If something is good, do everything in your power to further it; if something is bad, do everything in your power to eradicate it."

Anti-Semitism grounded on emotion alone did not satisfy the Germans because it would merely find release in pogroms (as it had throughout European history) and not in a "final solution"—a removal of the problem *(Entfernung)*. The ancient name for this sort of thinking is "hubris." Psychologically it represents an inflation of the ego which confuses itself with Deity. The conscious mind loses touch with the whole sustaining background of its will, particularly the shadow. Hubris compensates for intolerable humiliation such as that endured by the Germans after World War One. The end is nearly always tragic.

The Germans began to clean house by attempting to eradicate incurably ill and deformed children, then mentally and physically handicapped adults. (The churches in this case made their protests felt and the campaign was attenuated.)[80]

The aged, the gravely ill, the feeble, the criminal—all who are unable or unwilling to take care of themselves, let alone be productive—why not get rid of them? They only lower the standard of living and the quality of life. If Jews, gypsies and homosexuals contaminate the living space, why not dispose of them and with them their sicknesses and their aberrations. (Today we have trouble bringing ourselves to execute even serial killers.) Jews were vermin

---

[80] See Arno J. Mayer, *Why Did the Skies Not Darken?*, pp. 382f.

to the Nazis. And how do you deal with vermin? The program was called *Judenrein*, "Jew-clean."

While the systematic hunting down, torture, humiliation and extermination of the Jews is terrible enough, there is, to me, something in the Holocaust still more terrible. It is to be found in the record of how some responded to inhuman pressures and what effect those responses may have had on their souls.

In September, 1942, the Nazis gave Chaim Rumkowski, Chairman of the Council of Jewish Elders of the Lodz Ghetto, a choice: hand over for deportation all the unproductive of the ghetto—the elderly, the sickly and children under ten years old (a total of 20,000) or witness the annihilation of the entire population. He handed them over.

Two months previously, in July, 1942, the same choice had been given Adam Czerniakow, the Nazi-appointed Eldest of the Jews of the Warsaw Ghetto, whose response was to take poison. The Nazis answered with the most intensive deportation in the history of the Holocaust: within three months, 310,000 Jews were sent to die in Treblinka.[81]

Another example: the death camp employee whose daily routine it was to shave the heads of the women in preparation for their final "shower." (The industrious Germans had uses for human hair if not for the heads that bore it.) How did our Jewish barber find it within himself to chat with and reassure his terrified patrons? Or those Jews who, for a "living," stoked the ovens with the bodies of their countrymen—they must have possessed an indomitable will to live. And, under the circumstances, is this indomitable will to live admirable or not? It must "terrify and baffle mankind . . . with a huge and ominous mystery of the degeneration of the human spirit."[82]

The cruelty of the kapos (prisoners, some of them Jews, who had

---

[81] See Alan Adelson and Robert Lapides, *Lodz Ghetto: Inside A Community Under Siege*, pp. 489f.
[82] Isaac Deutscher, quoted in Michael R. Marrus, *The Holocaust in History*, p. 9.

been appointed to positions of authority over other prisoners) sometimes rivaled that of the Nazis. The story is told how, in compliance with Nazi deportation orders, a Jewish policeman was attempting to tear a child away from its father. To the father's desperate pleas the policeman answered,

> What makes you think I'm human? Maybe I'm a wild beast. I have a wife and three children. If I don't deliver my five heads by five P.M., they'll take my children. Don't you see, I'm fighting for the life of my own kids?[83]

Many of those, having arrived at Auschwitz and been rousted from their cattle cars in the night, brutally separated from their families, sniffing the sweet smell of burning flesh (Was it possible? There *had* been rumors . . .), that same night slipped away quietly to their graves.

Those who died in the gas chambers, according to one Auschwitz survivor, were the lucky ones. Others were thrust into deep pits the size of large swimming pools.

> Prisoners [many of them Jews] what worked there poured gasoline over the live ones and the dead ones. And the fat from the burning bodies they scooped and poured again so everyone could burn better.[84]

The war criminal Fyodor Federenko, when asked at his trial what he thought about his Jewish victims, answered with unassailable logic, "They were thinking about themselves. I was thinking about myself."

The Holocaust warns us of what human beings can and will perpetrate upon one another unless we gain more consciousness.

But lest we think we can rid ourselves of Nazis, thus repeating the inflated, erroneous Nazi idea (that it is possible to eradicate the shadow), listen to this: a Nazi is alive in your heart.

---

[83] Alexander Donat, quoted in Lucy S. Dawidowicz, *The War Against the Jews,* p. 412.

[84] Art Spiegelman, *Maus II: A Survivor's Tale,* p. 72.

To find the Nazi you must first seek the Jew; they are never far apart. Somewhere someone is hiding the Jew, feeding her against regulations. She is weak, she is wounded. Seek her out. Where is she hiding, this most wounded part of yourself? You have detached yourself from her but she is crying, complaining, demanding, even obnoxious. If you listen carefully you may find her. It will be painful to witness her disease.

Take her in your arms, listen to her troubles, nurse her wounds, stay with her, never leave for very long. Let her infirmities and her sorrows penetrate you; let her inferiorities penetrate you. This will put you back in touch with the source of the wounding and dispel the evil. You will have hunted and exposed the Nazi. When the inferior is accepted, when what falls short is accepted, the Nazi is starved and weakened.

20

Death and Resurrection

But if Christ is preached as raised from the dead, how can some among you say there is no resurrection of the dead? If there is no resurrection of the dead, then neither has Christ been raised. And if Christ has not been raised, then empty is our preaching; empty, too, your faith. . . . If for this life only we have hoped in Christ, we are the most pitiable people of all.

But in fact Christ has been raised from the dead, the first fruits of those who have fallen asleep. For since death came through a human being, the resurrection of the dead came also through a human being. For just as in Adam all die, so too in Christ shall all be brought to life, but each one in proper order: Christ the first fruits; then, at his coming, those who belong to Christ. . . .

But someone may say, "How are the dead raised? With what kind of body will they come back?" You fool! What you sow is not brought to life unless it dies. And what you sow is not the body that is to be but a bare kernel of wheat, perhaps, or of some other kind; but God gives it a body as he chooses, and to each of the seeds its own body. . . .

So it is with the resurrection of the dead. What is sown is perishable, what is raised is imperishable. It is sown in dishonor, it is raised in glory. It is sown in weakness, it is raised in power. It is sown a physical body, it is raised a spiritual body. If there is a physical body, there is also a spiritual body. So, too, it is written, "The first man, Adam, became a living being," the last Adam a life-giving spirit. But the spiritual was not first; rather the natural and then the spiritual. The first man was from the earth, earthly; the second man from heaven. As was the earthly one, so also are the earthly, and as is the heavenly one, so also are the heavenly. Just as we have borne the image of the earthly one, we shall also bear the image of the heavenly one. I tell you this, brethren: flesh and blood cannot inherit the kingdom of God, nor does the perishable inherit the imperishable.

Lo! I tell you a mystery. We shall not all die, but we shall all be changed, in a moment, in the twinkling of an eye, at the last trumpet.

For the trumpet will sound, and the dead will be raised imperishable, and we shall be changed. For this perishable nature must put on the imperishable, and this mortal nature must put on immortality. When the perishable puts on the imperishable, and the mortal puts on immortality, then shall come to pass the saying that is written: "Death is swallowed up in victory." "O death, where is thy sting? O grave, where is thy victory?"[85]

Just as the myth of death and resurrection is central to Christianity so also is it central to the new religion and the Jungian myth. The "sting" is withdrawn from death if, like Christ, we can say, "I have finished the work that you gave me to do."[86] This we can say if we have traveled along the path of individuation. We are speaking of literal death now, the most common Christian perspective. Depth psychology, however, also understands death and resurrection symbolically—as a cycle repeating itself innumerable times during a person's lifetime.

Paul asserts in the above passage that belief in resurrection is central to Christianity. He makes a comparison between Adam and Christ. Adam is the natural man who symbolizes us as formed by our childhood experiences—complexes and all. Christ is the natural man with the admixture of spirit who symbolizes the individuated human being: one who has succeeded to some degree in throwing off the shackles of the childhood complexes for the sake of truth and love. By permitting the Holy Ghost (the spirit of truth) to work through him, Christ was the first to overcome his complexes sufficiently to become the person God meant him to be. But Christ is only the first fruits of this work of coming to birth as a full human being. We all have this potential which in the coming age we are obliged to realize as much as we can.

Paul informs us that what is reborn is of a different nature than

---

[85] 1 Cor. 15:12-55, New American Bible.
[86] John 17:4.

what has died. In a successful analysis, too, what replaces the patient's myth or complex is different in nature from the original. By penetrating to the source of the wounding and abiding there, a process of transformation is initiated whose effects are quite unpredictable.

That is why Paul speaks of the last Adam (who is Christ) as a life-giving spirit. It is said that "the wind [spirit] bloweth where it listeth."[87] Inheritance of the spirit, Paul teaches, is a natural next step in our evolution. First must come the earthly, only then the spiritual. Humanity has taken possession, in some ways rather rudely, of the earth. The time is now ripe for the spirit to take possession of humanity.

Finally, Paul tells us that the fundamental condition of human nature is not death but change—change from the natural to the spiritual, from being caught up in our complexes to living in the light of love and truth. In overcoming our complexes through the grace of God we achieve, mysteriously, a kind of immortality, because in some part of us we have transcended flesh and blood—the flesh of our earthly, complex-ridden nature and the compulsive acting out of our instincts.

Without the intervention of the heavenly, my childhood myth becomes my identity, stripped of which I feel like nothing. If one has been reduced to nothing one has suffered a death. After death there inevitably follows a new birth—this we know from observing the cycles of nature. This new birth, according to the Jungian myth, will be under the aspect of Truth, that is, in accordance with *reality,* which is, as we know from Scripture, another name for God.

You see, our childhood myths are out of tune with reality—that's why they force us to seek therapy. They must be replaced with myths more in harmony with reality—that is what we mean by truth.

Christ said, "To this end was I born . . . that I should bear wit-

---

[87] John 3:8.

ness unto the truth."[88] Some postmodernists, with Pilate, will reply, "Truth, what is that?" To them, all truth is relative and therefore of equal value. But when we have no highest value we lose touch with God. Some (like the postmodernists and deconstructionists) have descended the mountain (set themselves free of the dogmatic religions) only to lose their way in Sheol, the valley of death where no highest value exists.

---

[88] John 18:37.

21
Being "Born Again"

There was a man of the Pharisees, named Nicodemus, a ruler of the Jews:

The same came to Jesus by night, and said unto him, Rabbi, we know that thou art a teacher come from God: for no man can do these miracles that thou doest, except God be with him.

Jesus answered and said unto him, Verily, verily, I say unto thee, Except a man be born again, he cannot see the kingdom of God.

Nicodemus saith unto him, How can a man be born when he is old? can he enter the second time into his mother's womb, and be born?

Jesus answered, Verily, verily, I say unto thee, Except a man be born of water and of the Spirit, he cannot enter into the kingdom of God.

That which is born of the flesh is flesh; and that which is born of the Spirit is spirit.[89]

The question Nicodemus asks, "How, as an adult, can one be born again?" is of deep concern to depth psychotherapy. Our childhoods have determined the myths which dictate our very perceptions. How can we tear those myths or complexes out of our flesh, and what will be left if we should succeed? A rebirth is in order, but how might it come about?

We can begin by listening more attentively to the wounded child within, which generally has a soothing and healing effect—though it is painful too. Mysteriously, the child within can transform sufficiently to relieve us from the necessity of replaying our myths by unconsciously inflicting hurts upon ourselves and others—Freud's "repetition compulsion."

---

[89] John 3:1-6.

This may be considered the "water" part of Christ's prescription: daily attention to one's injured soul, locating the exact sources of one's childhood wounding and relating it to present feelings of hurt and anger—in other words, cleansing ourselves of the residue of the childhood complexes. This part of the process of rebirth I think of as Freudian.

The Jungian part corresponds to the "spirit" Christ speaks of. This part of the work is airy, like the wind. It can go anywhere and see to the far reaches of the earth and to the end of time. It sees the purpose and the meaning of things. It provides us with a goal and shows us our path. Religions once gave us access to spirit as well as caring for our souls. They no longer do for most of us. We are in a time of transition between living religions. The Jungian myth, with consciousness as its central value, psychotherapy as its central ritual, and the child archetype as its initial symbol, is posited as the new world religion, so new it has only just quickened in its mother's womb.

22
Individuation and the Bible

Do not suppose that I have come to bring peace to the earth: it is not peace I have come to bring, but a sword. For I have come to set a man against his father, a daughter against her mother, a daughter-in-law against her mother-in-law. A man's enemies will be those of his own household. Anyone who prefers father or mother to me is not worthy of me. Anyone who prefers son or daughter to me is not worthy of me. Anyone who does not take his cross and follow in my footsteps is not worthy of me. Anyone who finds his life will lose it; anyone who loses his life for my sake will find it.[90]

In this paragraph Christ is embodying individuation. He is saying that individuation is not a peaceful process because it puts us into conflict with everything we thought we stood for. Neither is it a comfortable process, because we are never permitted the illusion that we are in possession of the truth.

New levels of truth seem constantly to be disclosing themselves as we evolve toward our authentic selves.

The family members referred to in this passage should be understood as *inner personalities*. While in the process of individuation, conflict with the actual mother or father is possible, conflict with the inner or introjected parent (for example, the mother's critical voice), is inevitable. So far as individuation is concerned one's enemies are those parental introjects. Nothing is closer to us than those inner voices and images—so close we confuse them with ourselves. And to the extent that one cannot extricate oneself from those introjects, one cannot claim one's authentic Self, that is, one cannot follow Christ, the first individuated person.

---

[90] Matt. 10:34-39, Jerusalem Bible.

The first thing some patients want to do (particularly young people) as they begin to shed their neuroses is to try to help their families. Usually this cannot be accomplished directly. But the fact that one family member (the young patient for instance) is able to extricate him- or herself from the family myth or neurosis can have a powerful liberating effect on the others.

The cross symbolizes the union of opposites. Reconciling the opposites (good and evil, matter and spirit, masculine and feminine, etc.) requires consciousness. To take up one's cross and follow Christ means to take up the burden of awareness of the opposites and follow the path of individuation.

Christ tells us that whoever follows ego exclusively will lose soul, which means that person will lose access to the unconscious, the factor that provides for the continuing regeneration and renewal of ego life. Hence the person who is capable of relativizing ego concerns—putting the ego in the service of the Self (God)—will find eternal renewal and rebirth. This is one meaning of Christ's resurrection: accepting the death of our will (in some regards) makes room for a new, more adequate attitude to be born in us to replace the outworn, willful approach that no longer serves life.

I have often cited Christ's words to my patients because so many find themselves in thrall to family members, or to their inner representations (introjects). This is equivalent to worshipping a false god. As children we naturally see our parents as the highest value, as gods, but so long as we persist in this we remain children, seeing God and the world "through a glass darkly." As long as we remain in the grip of childhood complexes, our vision remains obscured and parts of our nature unrealized.

What must occur is a death and resurrection event; not a literal death, but the sacrifice of one's myth or central complex—which feels like a death. Bringing about the dissolution of the myths imposed upon us in childhood is the preoccupation of depth psychotherapy. The rebirth part takes care of itself. In the words of the *I Ching,* the Chinese book of wisdom, "That a new beginning follows after every ending is the course of heaven."[91] This is equivalent to Christ's words, quoted above: "Anyone who loses his life for my sake will find it."

Loss of one's life for Christ's sake means, psychologically, giving up one's childhood myth for the purpose of individuation. It means disloyalty to one's parents for the sake of a higher loyalty, to God. In fact we only *can* give up our childhood loyalties for a higher purpose.

---

[91] Richard Wilhelm, trans., *The I Ching or Book of Changes,* p. 478.

23

Jung and the Bible on Love

One of the ways God breaks through into consciousness is through love. In the Bible we read:

> If I speak in the tongues of men and of angels, but have not love, I am a noisy gong or a clanging cymbal. And if I have prophetic powers, and understand all mysteries and all knowledge, and if I have all faith, so as to remove mountains, but have not love, I am nothing. If I give away all I have, and if I deliver my body to be burned, but have not love, I gain nothing. Love is patient and kind; love is not jealous or boastful; it is not arrogant or rude. Love does not insist on its own way; it is not irritable or resentful; it does not rejoice at wrong, but rejoices in the right. Love bears all things, believes all things, hopes all things, endures all things. Love never ends; as for prophecy, it will pass away; as for tongues, they will cease; as for knowledge, it will pass away. For our knowledge is imperfect and our prophecy is imperfect; but when the perfect comes, the imperfect will pass away. When I was a child, I spoke as a child, I understood as a child, I thought as a child: but when I became a man, I put away childish things. For now we see through a glass, darkly; but then face to face: now I know in part; but then shall I know even as also I am known. So faith, hope, love abide, these three; but the greatest of these is love.[92]

Love accomplishes what nothing else can—it commits us totally. This is terrifying. Perhaps that is why love must be as strong as death. Only something so strong and so beautiful could overcome our cowardice and our "realism."

It is terrifying to love someone because in so doing we feel as if we relinquish control over our destiny. In fact only in the service of love do we function at full capacity. We see more clearly because we have ceased serving the lesser gods of our complexes.

---

[92] 1 Cor. 13:1-13, Revised Standard Version (slightly modified).

One of Jung's early cases, startling in its success and notoriety, launched him upon his career as an independent practitioner: He was teaching at the University of Zurich when an old woman, crippled for seventeen years, appeared one day before his hypnosis seminar to serve as a subject. So talkative and tangential was she that Jung abruptly terminated the preliminary interview by declaring his intention to hypnotize her. Just as abruptly she closed her eyes and fell into a profound hypnotic trance without another word being spoken. Jung writes,

> I wondered at this, but did not disturb her. She went on talking without pause. . . . The situation was gradually growing rather uncomfortable for me. Here were twenty students present, to whom I was going to demonstrate hypnosis!
>
> After half an hour of this, I wanted to awaken the patient again. She would not wake up. I became alarmed; it occurred to me that I might inadvertently have probed into a latent psychosis. It took some ten minutes before I succeeded in waking her. All the while I dared not let the students observe my nervousness. When the woman came to, she was giddy and confused. I said to her, "I am the doctor, and everything is all right." Whereupon she cried out, "But I am cured!" threw away her crutches, and was able to walk. Flushed with embarrassment, I said to the students, "Now you've seen what can be done with hypnosis!" In fact I had not the slightest idea what had happened.[93]

Jung later discovered that this woman's mentally ill son had once been a patient on his ward. He was her only child of whom she had naturally cherished great expectations. Jung, on the other hand, was a young doctor just embarking on his career.

> I represented everything she had hoped her son might become. Her ambitious longing to be the mother of a hero therefore fastened upon me. She adopted me as her son, and proclaimed her miraculous cure far and wide.[94]

---

[93] *Memories, Dreams, Reflections,* p. 118.
[94] Ibid., p. 119.

This could be labeled a transference cure; nevertheless it represents a genuine healing, one which could be said to illustrate the power of love. Only for a value (in this case love of Jung) greater than the secondary gains accruing to the illness can the "myth" and the "habit" of the illness be given up. I believe love can be considered to play a part in every successful healing. As Jung writes elsewhere,

> Nothing is possible without love, not even the processes of alchemy, for love puts one in the mood to risk everything and not to withhold important elements.[95]

Ralph Waldo Emerson said, "When half-gods go, / The gods arrive"[96]—but the reverse is also true: when God arrives then the half-gods or false gods depart. Only a love greater than the love of the parents has the power to displace the love that keeps us children.

In earlier times this greater love or higher value generally took a religious turn, love of the *highest* value which is, by definition, love of God. Initiation into Church membership once signified that one had graduated from one's family of origin into full membership in "the family of man." Rites such as bar mitzvahs and confirmations once had the effect of releasing the young people from the constricting effect of the family complexes. It is an experience of this nature that the so-called men's movement seeks.

The presence of God and the availability of an authentic initiation process are the reasons why, despite the abusive conditions (as we now call them) under which children often grew up in former times, they probably grew up psychically healthier. In medieval times, for example, what children didn't get from parents they received perhaps from the extended family or lacking that from the family of man, the Church. The pervasive presence of God in the atmosphere of that time could and did compensate for childhood wounds and bestow a sense of worth and dignity upon each person.

---

[95] *C.G. Jung Speaking,* p. 404.
[96] "Give All to Love," stanza 4, in *The Portable Emerson,* p. 327.

Today the greater love or higher value once associated with God is more likely to be related to a person or (less often) an idea or principle. This is one reason why the love relationship is so problematic in our day; the highest value, God, is projected upon our lover. This is too heavy a burden for any human relationship to bear.

Let me close this section by giving the last word to Jung:

Love has more than one thing in common with religious faith. It demands unconditional trust and expects absolute surrender. Just as nobody but the believer who surrenders himself wholly to God can partake of divine grace, so love reveals its highest mysteries and its wonder only to those who are capable of unqualified devotion and loyalty of feeling. And because this is so difficult, few mortals can boast of such an achievement. But, precisely because the truest and most devoted love is also the most beautiful, let no man seek to make it easy. He is a sorry knight who shrinks from the difficulty of loving his lady. Love is like God: both give themselves only to their bravest knights.

I would offer the same criticism of trial marriages. The very fact that a man enters into a marriage on trial means that he is making a reservation; he wants to be sure of not burning his fingers, to risk nothing. But that is the most effective way of forestalling any real experience. You do not experience the terrors of the Polar ice by perusing a travel-book, or climb the Himalayas in a cinema.

Love is not cheap—let us therefore beware of cheapening it! All our bad qualities, our egotism, our cowardice, our worldly wisdom, our cupidity—all these would persuade us not to take love seriously. But love will reward us only when we do. I must even regard it as a misfortune that nowadays the sexual question is spoken of as something distinct from love. The two questions should not be separated, for when there is a sexual problem it can be solved only by love. Any other solution would be a harmful substitute. Sexuality dished out as sexuality is brutish; but sexuality as an expression of love is hallowed. Therefore, never ask what a man does, but how he does it. If he does it from love or in the spirit of love, then he serves a god; and whatever he may do is not ours to judge, for it is ennobled.[97]

---

[97] "The Love Problem of a Student," *Civilization in Transition,* CW 10, pars. 232ff.

24

New Life in Late Life

Now the Lord said to Abram, "Go from your country, and your kindred and your father's house to the land that I will show you." . . . So Abram went, as the Lord had told him. . . . Abram was seventy-five years old.[98]

The Bible sometimes assists in life transitions. This story of an old man obliged to leave the comforts of home and family to begin a new life depicts a secret current in the psyche which requires us, at any age, to open ourselves to new ideas—even to a new identity.

Like Abram I have been called upon to learn new tricks in old age. I lived my first sixty plus years under the aspect of the myth of the "suffering servant."[99] This provided me an identity, albeit a painful one. I identified with Christ, "My kingdom is not of this world." Yet events contrived to bind me to this world. My love for one who loves life pulled me into life. Money, taxes, investments, insurance, home repair—all life-sustaining, but for me, alas, soul-depleting.

I realized I could no longer hide behind my distaste for practical affairs and the story of Abraham lent me courage to develop a new attitude to practical life. If Abraham and Sarah could experience new birth in old age, so could I. It seems to be God's will that we go on changing. When that process ceases, when we notice with a shock that the world has suddenly evolved into something alien, then we begin to die.

Jung had something to say about this:

---

[98] Gen. 12:1-4; Revised Standard Version.
[99] See above, pp. 51ff.

I have treated many old people, and it's quite interesting to watch what the unconscious is doing with the fact that it is apparently threatened with a complete end. It disregards it. Life behaves as if it were going on, and so I think it is better for an old person to live on, to look forward to the next day, as if he had to spend centuries, and then he lives properly. But when he is afraid, when he doesn't look forward, he looks back, he petrifies, he gets stiff and he dies before his time. But when he's living and looking forward to the great adventure that is ahead, then he lives, and that is about what the unconscious is intending to do.[100]

---

[100] "Face to Face" interview, in *C.G. Jung Speaking*, p. 438.

25
A Psychological Gloss on a Benediction

The Lord bless you and keep you:
The Lord make his face to shine upon you, and be gracious to you:
The Lord lift up his countenance upon you, and give you peace.[101]

With these words the fathers of Israel were instructed by God to bless the children. The psychoanalyst Heinz Kohut saw that the child's discovery of the "gleam in his mother's eye" directed toward himself is a key ingredient of self-esteem. The beaming face of the parent fortifies the child against the inevitable failures, disappointments and rejections of life.

This is blessing indeed.

---

[101] Num. 6:24-26.

26

The Problem of Prayer

[Prayer] was and still is a problem for me. Some years ago I felt that all demands which go beyond what *is* are unjustified and infantile, so that we shouldn't ask for anything that is not granted. We can't remind God of anything or prescribe anything for him, except when he tries to force something on us that our human limitation cannot endure.[102]

For Jung prayer is legitimate only when the Self tries to force something upon the ego that the ego cannot stand. Then the ego may inform the Self of its human limitations. What this implies is that the Self can and will force ideas on the ego.

Such an instance is recorded by Jung, who writes of a man who believed he had cancer despite assurances to the contrary from his doctors. He said, "I know I do not have cancer but I think I have cancer." Jung observed:

I would tell him: "Yes, my friend, you are really suffering from a cancer-like thing, you really do harbour in yourself a deadly evil. However, it will not kill your body, because it is imaginary. But it will eventually kill your soul. . . . So that in the end you will not be a human being any more, but an evil destructive tumour."[103]

Jung writes that to tell this man that he was imagining he had cancer would be demoralizing. "It is far better for him to understand that his complex is an autonomous power directed against his conscious personality."[104]

I read this as stating that the complex is directed against the ego

---

[102] Jung, *Letters,* vol. 2, p. 120.
[103] "Psychology and Religion," *Psychology and Religion,* CW 11, par. 19.
[104] Ibid., par. 26.

by the Self. I think Jung is implying that all our complexes are like that. Elsewhere Jung has noted that the unconscious is ambivalent about consciousness. God sends Moses on a mission to Pharaoh and then seeks to kill him.[105] He is saved by his wife Zipporah. Similarly, God orders Balaam to obey the summons of the Moabite king and defend the Israelites before him. No sooner does Balaam pack his donkey and set out on his way than the angel of the Lord is dispatched to murder him on the road. His donkey senses danger and saves Balaam's life.[106] Again, God forces the pious Hosea to marry a prostitute.[107]

From a Jungian standpoint the Self is a mixture of opposites. Religion and psychology agree that things go better with us if we maintain a connection to a Greater Power. Prayer activates that connection which Jungian psychology calls the ego-Self axis.

Edward Edinger equates prayer with active imagination. It can take various forms: writing, drawing, painting, sculpting, dance or drama. Example: drawing an image from a dream or writing down a dialogue with a dream figure. Some forms of active imagination (for instance painting) result in a permanent record of the dialogue with the unconscious, which tangible record often continues to exert a stimulating effect upon consciousness.

Of prayer Edinger writes,

> It is not a request for anything specific. It is a request that the unconscious reveal itself with an image of some kind which can then lead to a dialogue. . . . Also I consider it legitimate to ask for help in time of need if one does not specify what it is. I think consulting the *I Ching* in times of uncertainty is a kind of prayer, for instance.[108]

Here is an example of prayer that yielded unexpected results:
A patient told me how she had prayed for the safety of her thir-

---

[105] Exod. 4:24.
[106] Num. 22:23ff.
[107] Hos. 1:2.
[108] *The New God-Image: A Study of Jung's Key Letters Concerning the Evolution of the Western God-Image*, p. 97.

teen-year-old son during his absence on a hiking trip. It was not a particularly dangerous expedition, but the invitation had been unexpected and she had not had time to help him prepare for it, nor to prepare herself. Also he was an introverted, cautious and overprotected child who was hesitant and anxious about the excursion, sensitized by a previous expedition where he had narrowly escaped (he thought) serious injury. It was a big step for him to make this trip.

Midway through his absence the image suddenly appeared to her of falling to her knees and praying to God for his safety. She hadn't prayed in many years and didn't really pray this time. She realized a part of her resisted praying. What was it? With a shock she recognized something within wished for his death.

Why? Because if he were gone her continuing torment at feeling inadequate to the task of single parenthood would be ended. She saw that her son was growing up, becoming less dependent and that the door between them was swinging shut. Little time was left to make good as a parent. Her final grade was entered in the book—she had been a mediocre parent at best, she felt.

It took years for her to understand more fully what had been revealed to her by her "prayer." She began to see that her fear of losing her child should be understood symbolically. Without realizing it she had been holding on to him too tightly. She was psychologically merged with him and as he was beginning adolescence, she needed to begin to say good-bye, to "lose" him.

Related to this idea, she came to realize that she had projected her wounded child upon her son, and that image of herself is what she cared about, not the image of him as a separate person. In therapist's parlance this is called "narcissism," which in some of its guises mimics love. She had treated her son as her mother had treated her, ostensibly with loving devotion, actually with no awareness of trespassing upon the sovereignty of another soul.

Her own mother thought she loved her daughter and convinced my patient of it, too. The wounded child in my patient knew she was unloved, but that childhood knowledge had to be repressed for the sake of survival. Like so many abused children she unconsciously carried on the cycle of abuse, believing, as her mother had believed, that she was being loving. The prayer opened a door; it took her many years and the help of therapy to step through it, that is, to realize that what she had thought was love was self-delusion and to realize why she had not been as good a mother as she had hoped. Her increased self-knowledge helped relieve her child of a certain burden.

Jung's work comes to bear in allowing her to live with that recognition of error. From a Jungian point of view, the fact that she became conscious of it, emotionally as well as intellectually, redeems her. Even adult children benefit from every bit of insight on the part of their parents, even if it is never conveyed to them in words, even if they are separated by great distances—even if they are separated by death. As Jung writes,

> The boon of increased self-awareness is the sufficient answer even to life's suffering, otherwise it would be meaningless and unendurable.[109]

---

[109] *Letters*, vol. 2, p. 311.

27

Christ As a Model for Individuation

The life of Christ, understood psychologically, represents the vicissitudes of the Self as it undergoes incarnation in an individual ego.[110]

Christ . . . is the still living myth of our culture. He is our culture hero, who, regardless of his historical existence, embodies the myth of the divine Primordial Man, the mystic Adam.[111]

And she brought forth her first-born son, and wrapped him in swaddling clothes, and laid him in a manger; because there was no room for them in the inn.[112]

Our horror at being subjected to unfair treatment is reflected in our predominant myth, that of Jesus Christ, most virtuous of men, who suffered persecution while still in His mother's womb and undeservedly died a criminal's death. In between He was misunderstood, betrayed and treated with hostility and derision. For two thousand years we have projected that fate upon Jesus. Now we must take it back upon ourselves.

Edward Edinger informs us that the familiar Biblical narrative of the Nativity can be understood psychologically as the birth of the Self, that is, the individuation process (the incarnation of God). He interprets Christ's birth among the animals as signifying that "the coming of the Self is an instinctual process, a part of living nature rooted in the biology of our being."[113] That there was "no room in the inn" tells us that the more differentiated, more civilized places in the psyche don't have a place for the individuation process.

---

[110] Edward F. Edinger, *The Christian Archetype*, p. 15.
[111] *Aion*, CW 9ii, par. 69.
[112] Luke 2:7.
[113] *The Christian Archetype*, p. 34.

But who among us would want to emulate Christ? Many worthy people in religious life have chosen to live a life in *imitatio Christi*. But it is just as authentic to imitate Christ by picking up one's own cross and living one's own life in this world, taking seriously the world's values (like "success") and struggling to reconcile them with the inner values.

Christ took our sins upon Himself. He showed us the way. We must now carry our own cross. This means that we must drink the bitter cup of our shortcomings down to its very dregs. We must accept and face our faults, as minor as they may seem compared to our neighbor's. It is not enough to recognize intellectually that we have shortcomings. In order for psychic transformation to occur, our very bones must feel remorse; our faults then become "a moral problem that challenges the whole ego-personality."[114]

---

[114] "The Shadow," *Aion,* CW 9ii, par. 14.

28
Reason and Statistics

That is the great problem before us today. *Reason alone no longer suffices.*[115]

Every human character occurs only once in the whole history of human beings.[116]

In his last years Jung was preoccupied with the subjects of synchronicity[117] and the incarnation of God in man. Both these ideas have the effect of liberating us from the oppressive and devaluing grip of causality (nineteenth-century science) and materialism, which inform us that we are victims of circumstances and of negligible importance in ourselves.

Science, though it is only a tool, has for the last two hundred years functioned as a god (a supreme value), exacting, as all gods do, worship in its service. Now we are at the point of emerging from an unconscious and conscious subservience to a science inclined to statistical formulations, thereby nullifying the essential quality of uniqueness in each individual. Admittedly science, even in its primarily mechanistic manifestation, stands as a bastion of reason in a time of disorientation. Yet we must be wary of a science whose materialistic/positivistic bias has come to stand for the denial of the grandeur of the individual.

Jung writes:

---

[115] "The Undiscovered Self," *Civilization in Transition,* CW 10, par. 574.

[116] Isaac Bashevis Singer, *Love and Exile,* p. xxix.

[117] Synchronicity = simultaneity + meaning. Synchronicity functions in the inner world as cause and effect functions in the outer world. (See "Synchronicity: An Acausal Connecting Principle," *The Structure and Dynamics of the Psyche,* CW 8)

Man is not complete when he lives in a world of statistical truth. He must live in a world where the whole of man, his entire history, is the concern, and that is not merely statistics. It is the expression of what man really is, and what he feels himself to be.

The scientist is always looking for an average. Our natural science makes everything an average, reduces everything to an average; yet the truth is that the carriers of life are individuals, not average numbers. When everything is statistical, all individual qualities are wiped out, and that, of course, is quite unbecoming. In fact, it is unhygienic, because if you wipe out the mythology of a man, his entire historical sequence, he becomes a statistical average, a number; that is, he becomes nothing.[118]

---

[118] Richard I. Evans, ed., *Jung on Elementary Psychology: A Discussion Between C.G. Jung and Richard I. Evans*, p. 153.

29
Self-Knowledge Gives Meaning to Life

Christ is the inner man who is reached by the path of self-knowledge.[119]

Reading the Biblical narrative of Christ's passion and coming upon the words, "Knowing everything that was going to happen to him . . . ,"[120] I wondered, "Why make a point that Jesus knows what will happen to him?" I thought of how knowledge was being emphasized here and how with my patients I emphasize awareness. I often have to assure them that it is through increased awareness that ninety per cent of the task of psychotherapy (that is, psychic transformation) is accomplished.

I can trace back my lifelong obsession with improving myself to my tenth year, and it probably goes back farther than that. Evidently I have felt inadequate for a long time. Why? The conclusion I have arrived at is that for a child of religious temperament to be born in America in the middle of the twentieth century must have been a dreadful shock.

As my schoolbooks were fond of proclaiming, we were living in the Industrial Age; we should be grateful for our high standard of living; we were the "Arsenal of Democracy" or else the "Breadbasket of the Western World." History, geography and social studies were celebrations of materialism and reinforced, rather than counterbalanced, the marketplace values of the world outside the classroom. Truly there seemed no place for the spirit.

I thought too of how I rejected knowledge as a youth and even

---

[119] *Aion,* CW 9ii, par. 318.
[120] John 18:4, Jerusalem Bible.

into middle age. I realized only lately that I was right to reject the type of knowledge purveyed in schools in the middle of the twentieth century. As Jung pointed out, under the impact of the French Enlightenment the spirit has been degraded into mere intellect.[121]

But a knowledge that tells us what is to come is a different order of knowledge. Jesus reassures us that the Holy Spirit will make known the things to come.[122] This was the sort of knowledge I was interested in, but what was taught in schools in my youth concerned itself only with the behavior of physical entities. I dare say my teachers considered it to be pure, untainted by metaphysical influence, but for me it was devoid of meaning.

In the last two hundred years we have learned the extent to which we are like machines and like animals. Now it is time to learn in what ways we are also like gods.

---

[121] *Letters,* vol. 2, p. 468; also *Psychology and Alchemy,* CW 12, par. 178.
[122] John 16:13.

30
The Answer Lies Within

My kingdom is not of this world.[123]

The kingdom of heaven is like a treasure hidden in a field which someone has found; he hides it again, goes off happy, sells everything he owns and buys the field.[124]

Jung's commentary on the above lines is worth quoting at length:

> The aim of the great religions is expressed in the injunction "not of this world," and this implies the inward movement of libido into the unconscious. Its withdrawal and introversion create in the unconscious a concentration of libido which is symbolized as the "treasure." . . .
>
> . . . The soul is a personification of the unconscious, where lies the treasure, the libido which is immersed in introversion and is allegorized as God's kingdom. This amounts to a permanent union with God, a living in his kingdom, in that state where a preponderance of libido lies in the unconscious and determines conscious life. The libido concentrated in the unconscious was formerly invested in objects, and this made the world seem all-powerful. God was then "outside," but now he works from within, as the hidden treasure conceived as God's kingdom.[125]

Jung's message may be summarized in one sentence: "Man has a soul and there is a treasure buried in the field."

The field is individual, subjective experience. In our time it is thought to be of little value. The treasure is God, the highest value. Another way to say it is that if we live our life true to our inner ex-

---

[123] John 18:36.
[124] Matt. 13:44, Jerusalem Bible.
[125] *Psychological Types,* CW 6, pars. 423f.

perience, fully, sincerely and devotedly (as Jesus did), we will find redemption; psychologically speaking, we will be more complete, that is, individuated.

Everything we need is to be found within us. This is a truth that is hard to hold onto, partly because in America, the world's most extraverted society, we are constantly being assured that what we need lies outside of us—in the shopping center, church social hall, university and so on.

The pundits scratch their heads, wondering, "Why, when Americans are better off economically than they've ever been before, is the national mood so discontented?" No better answer exists than that found in Scripture:

> Man shall not live by bread alone, but by every word that proceeds from the mouth of God.[126]

Or, as Jung reminded us:

> [We have] forgotten why man's life should be sacrificial, that is, offered up to an idea greater than himself.[127]

---

[126] Matt. 4:4, Deut. 8:3, Revised Standard Version.
[127] "Psychology and Religion," *Psychology and Religion,* CW 11, par. 133.

31
Psychotherapy As Sabbath

If you bring forth what is in you, what you bring forth will save you; if you do not bring forth what is within you, what you do not bring forth will destroy you.[128]

You must give expression to what is most truly yourself. For instance, you may need to write or paint or work in the garden or sail or play tennis or change your profession or love someone even if it makes a fool of you. If you do not discover who you are and give expression to it, this may undermine your health. Cancer, for instance, can result when there is an insurmountable obstacle to individuation, as apparently happened in the case of Jung's father, a minister, who died at age fifty-two perhaps because he could not reconcile his faith with science.[129] One could say that Jung spent his life in an attempt to accomplish the task that defeated his father.

Now, how can you serve the individuation process? This really means, how can you serve God (because becoming yourself is serving God)? Do generally valid precepts exist?

Take a Sabbath, a time of rest, once a week even if only for fifteen minutes. Protect this Sabbath from the claims of work, children, spouse, parents and friends. When you enter your free and protected space for those minutes try to be open to what comes to you. You can think of it as meditation if you want, or perhaps you will feel the urge to write or paint or draw or dance or think or be sad or be angry or be in nature. Regularity in taking your Sabbath is essential, however, so body and soul will come to anticipate it and depend upon it.

---

[128] "The Gospel of Thomas," no. 70, in *Nag Hammadi Library*, p. 126.
[129] See Barbara Hannah, *Jung: His Life and Work*, p. 63.

For some the weekly psychotherapy hour now serves as a kind of Sabbath. At that appointed day and time the patient's thoughts turn inward as he or she pauses and asks, "Who am I that all this should have happened to me?" This question reflects a religious attitude, which carefully considers one's personal experience.

As a therapist, I feel I perform no more important function than to hold the therapy hour sacred, thereby affirming the dignity and worth of the inner world. I have a rule that unless I receive twenty-four hours' notice, patients are charged for the hour whether or not they make use of it. The apparent harshness of the rule is to help keep the therapy hour inviolable. The demands of the inner world are easily set aside because the unconscious speaks at first in whispers. The penalty for violating the Sabbath in Biblical times was death. The penalty was severe not only because of the weight given that commandment by our fathers, but because of the ease with which worldly matters take precedence over matters of the soul.

Cancellations are infrequent in my practice but one week I had two. I spoke to both patients briefly on the phone. The young man said that his long-awaited motorcycle was ready and he was anxious to pick it up. The young woman explained she had to take her mother to the hospital, and besides she had to work. When I next saw them I brought up the subject. And in discussing it I think they realized that there was at least one person in the world, their therapist, who believed that what went on inside of them was quite as important as their outer affairs.

I find I influence my patients to take their inner world more seriously because I take it seriously—not only in my words but in my life. So when I have such a rule as this, and when in addition I start my sessions on time and finish on time, my actions bear witness to my belief in the sanctity of the psychotherapeutic hour.

Some therapists think it reflects a healthy liberality of mind to, say, extend the hour when the patient is late, or to make last-minute changes in scheduling. But the message that comes across unconsciously is, I think, that the therapy hour must give way to worldly considerations; that is, Caesar's world is more important than God's.

And when patients consider cutting down the frequency of their appointments or terminating altogether, therapists are often loath to oppose their will, thinking they have no right to try to keep the patient in therapy. There are times, however, when patients need encouragement to set aside a regular time to attend to that depreciated and neglected part of themselves, "the least of these my brethren," that is so deserving of respect and consideration.

Think of it this way: the extraverted attitude focuses on the goal, an attitude which, while perfectly appropriate in its own domain, is not appropriate to the inner world, where activities characterizing the feminine spirit predominate: circumambulation, acceptance, patience. And as in the outer world, attention and devotion to the inner task is likely to be rewarded, one such reward being enhanced self-esteem.

In this dark age of the soul, we in the West have forgotten how to look at things with the inner eye. Not only has Jung called this one-sidedness to our attention but he has revisioned the subjective aspect of life in psychological terms which are acceptable to our reason. As it is written:

> For this commandment which I command thee this day, it is not hidden from thee, neither is it far off.
> It is not in heaven. . . .
> Neither is it beyond the sea. . . .
> But the word is very nigh unto thee, in thy mouth, and in thy heart, that thou mayest do it.[130]

In other words, observance of the Sabbath, or engagement in an equivalent activity such as psychotherapy which honors the inner world, allows us access to it. Therefore, as it is written, "Choose life, that both thou and thy seed may live."[131]

---

[130] Deut. 30:11-14.
[131] Deut. 30:19.

Finale

In this book I have attempted to delineate the new religion and the Jungian myth and to illustrate them mostly with passages from Jung and the Bible.

The central theme in these pages has been that of *consciousness* or *self-knowledge*, for as Clement of Alexandria says, "When a man knows himself he knows God."[132] The process of coming to know ourselves is termed *individuation,* the preeminent form of worship of and service to God in the new religion.

The primary institution now serving the process of individuation is *depth psychology* because of its capacity to generate consciousness. A possible initial theme of the new religion is the *wounded inner child* because it can open us up to the world within, that is, the realm of soul.

Jungian psychology is not the new religion, but it can fairly be called its foremost apostle.

---

[132] Above, p. 23.

Bibliography

Adelson, Alan, and Lapides, Robert. *Lodz Ghetto: Inside a Community Under Siege.* New York: Viking, 1989.

Adler, Gerhard. "Aspects of Jung's Personality and Work." In *Psychological Perspectives,* vol. 6, no. 1 (Spring 1975).

_____. *Studies in Analytical Psychology.* New York: G.P. Putnam's Sons, for the C.G. Jung Foundation for Analytical Psychology, 1966.

Bauer, Jan. *Alcoholism and Women: The Background and the Psychology.* Toronto: Inner City Books, 1982.

Dawidowicz, Lucy S. *The War Against the Jews.* New York: Bantam Books, 1975.

Edinger, Edward F. *The Aion Lectures: Exploring the Self in Jung's* Aion. Toronto: Inner City Books, 1996.

_____. *An American Jungian: Edward F. Edinger in Conversation with Lawrence Jaffe.* 3 videotapes. Produced and Directed by Dianne D. Cordic. Los Angeles, 1990.

_____. *The Creation of Consciousness: Jung's Myth for Modern Man.* Toronto: Inner City Books, 1984.

_____. *Ego and Archetype: Individuation and the Religious Function of the Psyche.* Boston: Shambhala Publications, 1992.

_____. *Lectures on Jung's* Aion. Audiotapes. C.G. Jung Institute of Los Angeles, 1988.

_____. *The New God-Image: A Study of Jung's Key Letters Concerning the Evolution of the Western God-Image.* La Salle, IL: Open Court, 1996.

_____. *Transformation of the God-Image: An Elucidation of Jung's* Answer to Job. Toronto: Inner City Books, 1992.

Emerson, Ralph Waldo. *The Portable Emerson.* Ed. Mark van Doren. New York: The Viking Press, 1946.

Evans, Richard I., ed. *Jung on Elementary Psychology: A Discussion Between C.G. Jung and Richard I. Evans.* New York: E.P. Dutton, 1976.

Gubitz, Myron B. "Amelek: The Eternal Adversary." In *Psychological Perspectives,* vol. 8, no. 1 (Spring 1977).

Hannah, Barbara. *Jung: His Life and Work.* New York: G.P. Putnam's Sons, 1976.

122

Jaffe, Lawrence W. *Liberating the Heart: Spirituality and Jungian Psychology.* Toronto: Inner City Books, 1990.

Johnson, Robert. *Inner Work.* San Francisco: Harper and Row, 1986.

_____. *The Double Animus: Two Stories.* Audiotape. San Diego, CA: San Diego Friends of Jung, Oct. 18, 1978.

Jonas, Hans. *The Gnostic Religion.* Boston: Beacon Press, 1958.

Jung, C.G. *C.G. Jung Speaking.* Ed. William McGuire and R.F.C. Hull. Princeton.: Princeton University Press, 1977.

_____. *The Collected Works* (Bollingen Series XX). 20 vols. Trans. R.F.C. Hull. Ed. H. Read, M. Fordham, G. Adler, Wm. McGuire. Princeton: Princeton University Press, 1953-1979.

_____. *Letters* (Bollingen Series XCV). 2 vols. Trans. R.F.C. Hull. Ed. Gerhard Adler and Aniela Jaffé. Princeton: Princeton University Press, 1975.

_____. *Memories, Dreams, Reflections.* Ed. Aniela Jaffé. New York: Random House, 1963.

_____. *The Visions Seminars.* Zurich: Spring Publications, 1976.

Marrus, Michael R. *The Holocaust in History.* Hanover: University Press of New England, 1987.

Mayer, Arno J. *Why Did the Skies Not Darken?* New York: Pantheon, 1988.

Meier, Levi. *Jewish Values in Jungian Psychology.* Lanham, MD: University Press of America, 1991.

Nag Hammadi Library. Ed. J. Robinson. San Francisco: Harper and Row, 1977.

Plato. *The Works of Plato.* Trans. B. Jowett. New York: Tudor Publishing Company, n.d.

Sheldrake, Rupert. *A New Science of Life: The Hypothesis of Formative Causation.* Los Angeles: Jeremy P. Tarcher, 1981.

Singer, Isaac Bashevis. *Love and Exile.* New York: Farrar, Strauss and Giroux, 1984.

Spiegelman, Art. *Maus II: A Survivor's Tale.* New York: Pantheon, 1991.

von Franz, Marie-Louise. *C.G. Jung: His Myth in Our Time.* Toronto: Inner City Books, 1998.

Wilhelm, Richard, trans. *The I Ching or Book of Changes* (Bollingen Series XIX). 3rd ed. Trans. into English by Cary F. Baynes. Princeton: Princeton University Press, 1967.

Wordsworth, William. *Poetical Works.* London: Oxford University Press, 1961.

Index

Studies in Jungian Psychology
by Jungian Analysts

Quality Paperbacks

Prices and payment in $US (except in Canada, and Visa orders, $Cdn)

Risky Business: Environmental Disasters and the Nature Archetype
Stephen J. Foster (Boulder, CO) ISBN 978-1-894574-33-4. 128 pp. $25

Jung and Yoga: The Psyche-Body Connection
Judith Harris (London, Ontario) ISBN 978-0-919123-95-3. 160 pp. $25

The Gambler: Romancing Lady Luck
Billye B. Currie (Jackson, MS) 978-1-894574-19-8. 128 pp. $25

Conscious Femininity: Interviews with Marion Woodman
Introduction by Marion Woodman (Toronto) ISBN 978-0-919123-59-5. 160 pp. $25

The Sacred Psyche: A Psychological Approach to the Psalms
Edward F. Edinger (Los Angeles) ISBN 978-1-894574-09-9. 160 pp. $25

Eros and Pathos: Shades of Love and Suffering
Aldo Carotenuto (Rome) ISBN 978- 0-919123-39-7. 144 pp. $25

Descent to the Goddess: A Way of Initiation for Women
Sylvia Brinton Perera (New York) ISBN 978-0-919123-05-2. 112 pp. $25

Addiction to Perfection: The Still Unravished Bride
Marion Woodman (Toronto) ISBNj 978-0-919123-11-3. Illustrated. 208 pp. $30/$35hc

The Illness That We Are: A Jungian Critique of Christianity
John P. Dourley (Ottawa) ISBN 978-0-919123-16-8. 128 pp. $25

Coming To Age: The Croning Years and Late-Life Transformation
Jane R. Prétat (Providence) ISBN 978-0-919123-63-2. 144 pp. $25

Jungian Dream Interpretation: A Handbook of Theory and Practice
James A. Hall, M.D. (Dallas) ISBN 978-0-919123-12-0. 128 pp. $25

Phallos: Sacred Image of the Masculine
Eugene Monick (Scranton) ISBN 978-0-919123-26-7. 30 illustrations. 144 pp. $25

The Sacred Prostitute: Eternal Aspect of the Feminine
Nancy Qualls-Corbett (Birmingham) ISBN 978-0-919123-31-1. Illustrated. 176 pp. $30

The Pregnant Virgin: A Process of Psychological Development
Marion Woodman (Toronto) ISBN 978-0-919123-20-5. Illustrated. 208 pp. $30pb/$35hc

Discounts: any 1-9 books, 20%; 10-19, 25%; 20 or more, 40% .

Add Postage/Handling: 1-2 books, $6 surface ($10 air); 3-4 books, $12 surface

($16 air); 5-9 books, $16 surface ($25 air); 10 or more, $16 surface ($30 air)

Visa credit cards accepted. Toll-free: Tel. 1-888-927-0355; Fax 1-888=924-1814.

INNER CITY BOOKS, Box 1271, Station Q, Toronto, ON M4T 2P4, Canada
Tel. (416) 927-0355 / Fax (416) 924-1814 / booksales@innercitybooks.net